W9-COV-595

Cross-References to the *Little English Handbook,*
Fourth Edition

Workbook Exercises	*Handbook Section*
Agreement of Subject and Verb	22
Verb Forms	33
Apostrophe for Possession	20
Individual or Joint Possession	20
its/it's; Contractions	21
Pronoun/Antecedent Agreement	23, 24
Dangling Verbals	25
Misplaced Modifiers	26
Parallel Words, Phrases, Clauses	27
Sentence Fragments	29
Comma Splice	30
Fused Sentence	31
Confusing Sentences	32, 45
Combining Sentences for Variety	pp. 86–100
Wrong Word/Faulty Predication	40
Precise and Appropriate Words	41, 42
Using Proper Idiom	43
Trite Expressions	44
Awkward Sentences	45
Wordiness	46, 47
Mixed Metaphor	48
Use of Active and Passive Voice	49
Unity in the Paragraph	50
Coherence in the Paragraph	51
Adequate Development of the Paragraph	52
Use of the Comma	60, 61, 62, 63, 64, 65
Use of the Semicolon	66, 67
Use of the Colon	68
Use of the Dash	69, 70, 71
Quotation Marks	80, 81, 82, 84
Italics (Underlining)	83, 85, 86
Hyphens	87, 88
Numbers	89
Capitalization	90
Research Paper: Source Evaluation	
Research Paper: Note-Taking	A, B, C
Research Paper: Incorporation of Notes	D, E
Research Paper: MLA Documentation	F, G, H, K, L, M
Research Paper: APA Bibliography Style	O

The Little English Workbook

Second Edition

Kathryn N. Benzel

Janne Goldbeck
Idaho State University

Michael Benzel
Kearney State College

Scott, Foresman and Company
Glenview, Illinois

Dallas, Tex.   Oakland, N.J.   Palo Alto, Cal.
Tucker, Ga.   London, England

Acknowledgments

Material from *Book Review Digest* is reproduced by permission of The H.W. Wilson
Company.   *BusinessWeek* cover logo, masthead, table of contents, and "Prime
Time Gets Even Costlier" reprinted from the July 26, 1982 issue of *BusinessWeek* by
special permission. Copyright © 1982 by McGraw-Hill, Inc.   Newton N. Minow,
from *Equal Time: The Private Broadcaster and the Public Interest*, edited by Lawrence
Laurent. Copyright © 1964 by Newton N. Minow. Reprinted with the permission of
Atheneum Publishers.   From "El Teatro Campesino, Its Beginnings" by Luis
Valdez from *Ramparts*, July 1966. Copyright © 1966, Ramparts Magazine, Inc.
Reprinted by permission of Bruce W. Stilson.   From *Language* by Edward Sapir.
Copyright 1921 by Harcourt Brace Jovanovich, Inc.; renewed 1949 by Jean K. Sapir.
Reprinted by permission of the publisher.   From *The Lives of a Cell* by Lewis
Thomas. Copyright © 1974 by Lewis Thomas. Originally published in *The New
England Journal of Medicine*. Reprinted by permission of Viking Penguin Inc. and
Penguin Books Ltd.   From *The Plug-In Drug* by Marie Winn. Copyright © 1977 by
Marie Winn Miller. Reprinted by permission of Viking Penguin Inc.   Excerpt
from "Snake Lore" from *The Foxfire Book* edited by Eliot Wigginton. Copyright ©
1969, 1970, 1971 by Southern Highlands Literary Fund, Inc. and Copyright © 1968,
1969, 1972 by Brooks Eliot Wigginton. Reprinted by permission of Doubleday &
Company, Inc.   From *Television: A Selection of Readings from TV Guide Magazine*
edited by Barry G. Cole. Copyright © 1970 by The Free Press, a Division of
Macmillan Publishing Company. Reprinted by permission.   From *Television and
Radio* edited by Poyntz Tyler, Reference Shelf Vol. 33, No. 6. Copyright © 1961 by
The H.W. Wilson Company. Reprinted by permission.   From *Television Fraud:
The History and Implications of the Quiz Show Scandals* by Kent Anderson. Copyright ©
1978 by J. Kent Anderson. Reprinted by permission of Greenwood Press.   From
"A Whalewatcher's Diary" by Gordon S. Hayward from *Blair & Ketchum's Country
Journal*, August 1977. Copyright © 1977 Country Journal Publishing Co., Inc.
Reprinted by permission.   From *Who's Who in America*, 42nd Edition. Copyright ©
1982 by Marquis Who's Who Incorporated. Reprinted by permission.

Preface to Second Edition

The previous edition of *The Little English Workbook* provided students a means of improving their writing through a series of self-contained exercises. The introductory explanations briefly outlined conventions of grammar, style, paragraphing, punctuation, and mechanics, and pinpointed common problems in these areas. The exercises which followed these explanations were designed to improve writing through concentrated drill on specific problems and by generating conventionally accepted patterns of writing (e.g., subject-verb agreement, pronoun use, comma use, and so on). In this second edition we have maintained these objectives but have updated some exercises, expanded others, added review exercises, and developed a research writing component. Still, in keeping with our original intention, we have made every effort to keep the *Workbook* as concise as possible.

New Exercises

With the expanded exercises, students will have more practice correcting problem areas. In particular, we have enlarged the **sentence combining** section in order to define sentence elements and to exemplify kinds of sentences. Some of these exercises ask students to purposely create compound and complex sentences using coordination, subordination, and modification. The new **review exercises** require students to revise and edit longer prose passages by applying their knowledge of particular problems to a larger context, one which simulates their own revising process. In this way, we hope students will gain confidence not only in their recognition of specific problems but also in their writing skills as a whole process.

Research Writing Exercises

One significant change from the first to second edition of *The Little English Workbook* is the addition of exercises on research paper writing. As more and more composition programs have begun to reintegrate a research paper component, these exercises are increasingly necessary in a composition workbook.

In devising the exercises, we followed three principles. First, the exercises are directly applicable to student needs. Our experience in teaching research writing has shown us that students need to be aware that there is a process behind building a research paper. Therefore, we simulate a research project. Students are presented with a topic and information from five sources on that topic. Their task is to evaluate the information, take notes, and write a paragraph using their notes. They are also given practice in constructing endnote and bibliography pages using either the MLA or APA style.

Second, the exercises reflect a **thesis** paper rather than a **report** paper. Students come to understand that a research paper can and should reflect their own thoughts, as based on careful analysis and evaluation of the topic and of sources of information on the topic; in other words, the research paper is more than just a report on a topic and thus is more than just a pastiche of quoted, paraphrased, and summarized material. So, in our exercises we have given students an argumentative thesis to support.

Finally, the exercises are "little" in keeping with the philosophy which governs the entire workbook; we have included only those exercises applicable to the simulated project approach and to documentation. These exercises on **Source Evaluation, Note Taking, Incorporation of Notes,** and **Documentation** guide students through these stages of writing a research paper.

Cross-Index and Solutions Manual

As a result of these changes, this second edition has become a more **self-sufficient textbook;** in particular, the addition of the research writing exercises adds a new dimension to the idea of a composition workbook. With fuller explanations, reordered grammar items, and more emphasis on sentence-related exercises, students will be able to use the *Workbook* without reference to other sources. Nonetheless, the *Workbook* still follows the philosophy, subject matter, and tone which make it complementary to Edward P.J. Corbett's *Little English Handbook.* We have therefore provided a handy cross-index to the *Handbook,* for more convenient reference to the applicable extended coverage. A solutions manual with answer keys and recommended procedures for the research writing section is available to instructors.

Acknowledgments

No project like this workbook can ever be completed successfully by the authors alone. We are indebted, as always, to our students who remain a source of inspiration. We would especially like to thank our reviewers, Stanley Kozikowski, Mary Sue Ply, John Presley, and Adam Sorkin, for their careful and copious notes and suggestions; their conscientious efforts have directed our revisions.

A special thanks goes to those people at Scott, Foresman who helped make this endeavor successful and rewarding: Amanda M. Clark for her support in initiating the second edition; Harriett Prentiss for her administrative expertise; Constance Rajala for her technical advice, continual editing, and practical suggestions; and Russell Schneck in the Design department who carefully constructed the research writing format.

Kathryn N. Benzel
Janne Goldbeck
Michael Benzel

Contents

PARAGRAPHING

PUNCTUATION

MECHANICS

Grammar

ITEM 22

AGREEMENT OF SUBJECT AND VERB

A simple sentence consists of a subject and a predicate containing a verb. The subject is a noun or noun equivalent, such as a pronoun, gerund, infinitive, or noun clause. The predicate contains a verb, which generally follows the subject, and often other qualifying structures (objects, complements, modifiers). Note the following examples; the subjects and verbs are labeled and the predicate is underlined.

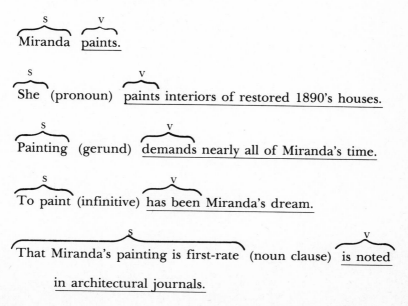

S V
Miranda paints.

S V
She (pronoun) paints interiors of restored 1890's houses.

S V
Painting (gerund) demands nearly all of Miranda's time.

S V
To paint (infinitive) has been Miranda's dream.

S V
That Miranda's painting is first-rate (noun clause) is noted

in architectural journals.

1

1 A verb agrees with its subject in person and number.

To be understood, you must make verbs **agree** with their subjects. Study the faults in the following sentences and note how they have been corrected. The subjects are underlined once; the verbs, twice.

He <u>run</u> the fastest mile in Ohio.

Rewrite:
He <u>runs</u> the fastest mile in Ohio.

<u>They</u> <u>runs</u> a fast two-mile relay.

Rewrite:
<u>They</u> <u>run</u> a fast two-mile relay.

In the above sentences notice the difference between the singular form of the verb **run** (runs) and the plural form (run). Most verbs ending in a single **s** (**looks, dresses, flies**) are singular. Most verbs not ending in **s** are plural. Note the following list of examples:

SINGULAR	PLURAL
he looks	they look
he goes	they go
he seems	they seem
he makes	they make
he tries	they try
he plays	they play

Decide which verb in parentheses agrees with the subject given and underline it.

1. students (ask, asks)

2. movies (appeal, appeals)

3. men (is, are)

4. plane (fly, flies)

5. Doris (eat, eats)

6. water (drip, drips)

7. chefs (cook, cooks)

8. grandmother (knit, knits)

9. players (shoot, shoots)

10. secretaries (type, types)

11. teams' locker room (is, are)

12. monkeys (climb, climbs)

13. bank teller (count, counts)

14. mountains (is, are)

15. logs (burn, burns)

2 There are some special situations involving the agreement of subject and verb.

A. Compound subjects
   1. Singular subjects joined by **and** take a plural verb.

<u>Susan and her brother</u> <u>run</u> six miles every day.
<u>A peaceful mind and a contented heart</u> <u>are</u> the group's goals.

   2. Singular subjects joined by **or** or by correlative conjunctions (**either . . . or, neither . . . nor**) take a singular verb.

<u>Susan or her brother</u> <u>runs</u> six miles every day.
<u>Neither Susan nor her brother</u> <u>runs</u> six miles every day.

   3. When both subjects are plural, the verb is plural.

<u>The brothers and sisters</u> <u>run</u> six miles every day.
<u>Either test scores or grades</u> <u>are</u> <u>used</u> on the application.

   4. When one subject is singular and the other is plural, and the subjects are joined by **or** or by correlative conjunctions (**either . . . or, neither . . . nor**), the verb agrees in number with the closest subject.

<u>Either the nurse or the doctors</u> <u>prescribe</u> the treatment.
<u>Neither the brothers nor the sister</u> <u>appears</u> to have run six miles.

B. Collective nouns as subjects
   1. If the collective noun considers the group as a unit, the verb is singular.

<u>Mathematics</u> <u>was</u> Frank's primary concern.
The <u>number</u> of recruits <u>has</u> <u>increased.</u>

   2. If the collective noun is considered as individuals of a group, the verb is plural.

The welcoming <u>committee</u> <u>want</u> to extend their greetings.
A <u>number</u> of recruits <u>have</u> <u>petitioned</u> for new living quarters.

   3. Common collective nouns

choir	group	media
committee	jury	series
economics	linguistics	team
faculty	mathematics	class

C. Expletive structures: **there is/are, there was/were**
   1. If the delayed or real subject following the expletive **there** is singular, the verb is singular; if the subject is plural, the verb is plural.

There <u>is</u> an <u>odor</u> of onions in the kitchen.
There <u>are</u> <u>Karen and John</u> coming down the lane.

NAME _____ DATE _____

Identify the subject of each sentence by underlining it. Is the verb singular or plural?

Example: **singular** The following reason is absurd.

_____ 1. The price of sugar is ridiculous.

_____ 2. The reasons for the quarrel are still unknown.

_____ 3. The dog and cat are running around the fence.

_____ 4. There are eighty tests on the desk.

_____ 5. The orchestra members are tuning their instruments.

_____ 6. Neither John nor Peter fails to yield the right of way.

_____ 7. The best of the apple trees has many blossoms.

_____ 8. Either the boss or his secretaries run the photocopier.

_____ 9. The reports of misdemeanors haven't arrived.

_____ 10. Yoga is a discipline that many try in order to soothe their nerves.

_____ 11. The contract concerning the updated items reduces the client's liability.

_____ 12. Budget planners for the city deny the major's charge.

_____ 13. Neither the first proposal nor the final decision reflects the major changes.

_____ 14. Health services provide the necessary forms.

_____ 15. Last summer's temperatures indicate a warming trend.

NAME _____ DATE _____

Write the correct present tense form of the verb in parentheses.

1. Pen and pencils (be) _____ handy items.

2. News of a car crash always (stun) _____ the television viewers.

3. Neither the players nor the coach (be) _____ happy.

4. Eight of the singers (have) _____ laryngitis.

5. The turtles and cat (get) _____ along quite well.

6. The new thousand-dollar bills (scare) _____ the bank manager.

7. The poetry of William Carlos Williams (introduce) _____ the Imagist movement.

8. Either John or his brothers (need) _____ money for school.

9. Tornadoes (scare) _____ me.

10. There (be) _____ three new band members.

11. Eighteen members of the team (be) _____ ill from last night's dinner.

12. Every year birds (fly) _____ non-stop to a remote spot in Peru.

13. The housing crisis facing Southern cities (be) _____ unprecedented.

14. The series of Shakespearean plays (open) _____ July 15.

15. The basketball team's lineup (include) _____ a seven-foot center.

3 Special structures

A. The following indefinite pronouns and other words can be singular or plural depending on their contexts: **each, either, neither, one, everyone, everybody, no one, nobody, anyone, anybody, someone, somebody, all, any, none**. Cues from the context, such as verb form or pronoun use or prepositional modifier, can help you decide whether they are singular or plural. Note the following examples:

<u>One</u> of the apples <u>is</u> ripe. (singular)
<u>Each student</u> <u>was</u> awarded a prize. (singular)
<u>All</u> of the cake <u>was</u> gone. (singular)
<u>None</u> of the final scores <u>were posted</u>. (plural)
<u>Someone</u> <u>was</u> <u>lurking</u> about the alley. (singular)

B. The following common words are plural: **several, few, both, many, some, any, none**. When the words **some, any, none**, and **all** are followed by a phrase, that phrase often helps you decide whether the words are singular or plural. Note the following examples:

<u>Some</u> of the pencils <u>are</u> dull. (plural)
<u>Some</u> of the food <u>was</u> frozen. (singular)

<u>All</u> of the tires <u>were</u> new. (plural)
<u>All</u> of the gasoline <u>was spilled</u>. (singular)

Note: Here **food** and **gasoline** in the prepositional phrases indicate a **mass** of something, and therefore, the **some** and **all** are to be construed as singular. **Pencils** and **tires** are **countable** items, and therefore, the **some** or **all** is to be construed as plural.

NAME _____ DATE _____

In the following sentences underline the subject once and the correct verb in parentheses twice.

1. (Is, Are) every one of these balls yours?

2. Neither of the students (were, was) afraid to work.

3. A few of the girls in my class (were, was) on the honor roll.

4. Some of the proposed legislation (was, were) withheld until the next session.

5. Everybody in the South (knows, know) what the Civil War was like.

6. Both of your brothers (is, are) in the Army.

7. A few of the newspaper articles (is, are) written by ghost-writers.

8. Every one of our berry bushes (was, were) uprooted by the storm.

9. Several of the debate team members (seems, seem) nervous.

10. Each of the apple trees (needs, need) pruning.

11. One of your conclusions (is, are) easily refuted.

12. Not one of these students (has, have) finished the required homework.

13. Several of the wines (was, were) given gold medals for excellence.

14. No one (know, knows) where the treasure (is, are) hidden.

15. Anybody within range of the planet (was, were) contaminated by the chemical explosion.

4   BE Verb

The BE verb has more distinct forms than other verbs in the English language. To be sure that you use this verb correctly, study the following examples:

PRESENT TENSE

	SINGULAR	PLURAL
1st person	I am	we are
2nd person	you are	you are
3rd person	he, she, it is	they are

SIMPLE PAST TENSE

	SINGULAR	PLURAL
1st person	I was	we were
2nd person	you were	you were
3rd person	he, she, it was	they were

PERFECT TENSE

	SINGULAR	PLURAL
1st person	I have been	we have been
2nd person	you have been	you have been
3rd person	he, she, it has been	they have been

PAST PERFECT TENSE

	SINGULAR	PLURAL
1st person	I had been	we had been
2nd person	you had been	you had been
3rd person	he, she, it had been	they had been

SIMPLE FUTURE TENSE

	SINGULAR	PLURAL
1st person	I will be	we will be
2nd person	you will be	you will be
3rd person	he, she, it will be	they will be

FUTURE PERFECT TENSE

	SINGULAR	PLURAL
1st person	I will have been	we will have been
2nd person	you will have been	you will have been
3rd person	he, she, it will have been	they will have been

PRESENT PARTICIPLE

being

PAST PARTICIPLE

been

NAME _____ DATE _____

Some of the following sentences use the *BE* verb properly; mark a *C* in the blank in those sentences. If the verb is incorrect, cross it out and write in the correct form.

1. She and her relatives are _____ hideous people, when they try to outdo each other.

2. That committee's decision are _____ forthright and far-reaching.

3. Clara, Dave's sister, is _____ afraid of riding roller coasters.

4. Bus depots be _____ dangerous, so police watch them carefully.

5. Great Britain were _____ America's greatest source for importing tobacco.

6. Bill went to Europe and be _____ ecstatic about the Louvre.

7. Once Mabel is removed from the hospital, she am _____ content.

8. The young pups were _____ hungry because their master hadn't returned to feed them.

9. Every Monday I are _____ happy because I can go to work.

10. Doing exercises every day are _____ healthful.

11. Many clients has been _____ worried by the sudden drop in sales.

12. Finally, you has been _____ given your just reward.

13. If he was _____ there, then you was _____ there, too.

14. Marcia and Sheila have been _____ seeking employment at large corporations.

15. Neither Joey nor Janice is _____ present for the final testing.

NAME _____ DATE _____

In each of the following sentences you must make a choice of verbs. Write the subject of each verb and then the correct verb form. Remember that the verb should agree in person and number with its subject.

Example: The rose bush with thorns (was, were) beautiful.
rose bush was

1. Both of the runners on our relay team (look, looks) good.

2. Fourteen of the twenty students (are failing, is failing) the final exam.

3. The bus for the football team (leave, leaves) at 9:00 A.M.

4. This best-selling novel for adults (make, makes) good reading.

5. The musicians in the orchestra (was, were) the most artistic.

6. The pine tree with wide-spreading branches (was brushing, were brushing) the roof.

7. The secretaries in the office (work, works) long hours.

8. Some guards from the pool (were trying, was trying) to calm the mothers.

9. The ships along the waterfront (seem, seems) to be anchored.

10. The sound of the storm (was, were) strange and frightening.

11. The generals (lecture, lectures) at colleges across the country.

12. Jonathan (argue, argues) his point successfully for the debate team.

13. The committee (welcome, welcomes) its new members.

14. The jar (contain, contains) exactly 437 jelly beans.

15. The movies (demonstrate, demonstrates) the horrible consequences of drug abuse.

NAME _____ DATE _____

Using all of the rules for subject-verb agreement, correct the following sentences if necessary. If the sentence is correct, mark a *C* next to it. If there is an error, circle the mistake and correct it.

1. Every one of us have earned a spot on the tennis team.

2. We all go swimming in Betty and Dennis's pool.

3. Everyone wants to do something if it's *in*.

4. Do you think Joyce want those old chairs in the basement?

5. One of the secretaries' excuses for being tardy are really farfetched.

6. Either the mice or the cat find the way out.

7. Many of the pies has been burned.

8. Some of the pasta in this bowl are not done.

9. Please give Denise her snack when she come home.

10. Until I confront an issue I don't realize the problems involved.

11. She been still dressing when I arrived.

12. Building log cabins were hard work for the young couple.

13. Martha and her sisters feels like they've been to Alaska and back.

14. The piano tuner, who lives in Spokane, only tunes pianos on weekends.

15. The mountain bluebird of the Rockies display a spectacular color.

16. Do you think Grandma like the apron I made her?

17. Learning about writing sometimes seem like a boring, hopeless task.

18. Are one of those boxes small enough?

19. Each of the races is sure to be close.

20. If you loses your money in Las Vegas, don't come to see me.

21. The wildflowers of the Northwest is beautiful.

22. In order to sublet the apartment, the renters were to give the manager notice.

23. The teacher and the new student argues continually about transfer credits.

24. A new suit of clothes cost about $150.

25. The manager of the night clubs say he will not have live entertainment.

26. The spouses was invited to the Sunday brunch.

27. The beginning of the Olympic Games were postponed.

28. The risks involved were too dangerous for the new pilot.

29. A story's beginning spark the reader's curiosity.

30. A referee settles disputes.

31. This region's economic development are poorly conceived by the new commerce board.

32. The volleyball teams are staying in the hotel on the beach.

33. You have seen the New England-style cottage on the old road, haven't you?

34. The tribe's quest for youth were central to their beliefs.

35. The thoughts and insights of the philosopher are phenomenal.

Edit the following passage for subject-verb agreement.

TELEVISION: A MODERN DILEMMA

With all the devices for entertainment, people of the twentieth century has become passive. Television, the primary form of today's entertainment, does not provide people with the excitement to challenge or motivate. Actually TV only point out the absurdities of modern living—disaster in the news and in melodrama; that's a poor motivation for challenge.

But why exactly do modern people become so attached to TVs? The answer is simple, if people will admit it. People looks passively at the world; someone or something else have to be active. The way in which people watches TV is the way they view the world around them. Why go play football with the neighborhood kids when TV show the "pros" at work? Why try to stop crime in neighborhoods when the Hill Street police can do it?

Unfortunately this passive attitude of today's people have affected not only their involvement in the world but also their self-images. "Someone else can take care of it" is their response. But, by continually saying this, people is put in a position that do not allow them to reveal their expertise or to feel satisfaction from reward. If someone else always do it, how can an individual gains a sense of self-worth? And worse yet, once this state of inactivity occur people usually sits back even farther in their easy chairs.

Grammar

VERB FORMS

Although many errors involving verbs result from the lack of agreement between subject and predicate (see Item **22**), verb errors also occur because of improper past tense and past participle forms. This problem is particularly troublesome when verb tenses shift in paragraphs; the reader can misinterpret easily the chronological organization.

There are two past tense forms with which you need to be familiar—simple past tense and those past tense forms which require both an auxiliary verb and a past participle. Note the changes in the following verb:

Present tense	she plays
Past tense	she played
Past participle	she has (had) played

The basic rule regarding past tense and past participle forms of regular verbs is that they are formed by adding **-ed**, **-d**, or **-t** to the verb stem (e.g., walk—walked, believe—believed, build—built). In cases where you are unsure of a past tense or past participle form of an irregular verb, you should consult a dictionary. For your reference a list of the most often used irregular verbs and their past tense and past participle forms follows.

STEM FORM	PAST TENSE	PAST PARTICIPLE
begin	began	begun
bite	bit	bitten
blow	blew	blown
break	broke	broken
choose	chose	chosen
do	did	done
drink	drank	drunk
drive	drove	driven
eat	ate	eaten
fall	fell	fallen
fly	flew	flown
forget	forgot	forgotten
give	gave	given
go	went	gone
know	knew	known
lay	laid	laid
lie	lay	lain
pay	paid	paid
ride	rode	ridden
ring	rang	rung
rise	rose	risen
run	ran	run
see	saw	seen
sit	sat	sat
speak	spoke	spoken
swear	swore	sworn
take	took	taken
throw	threw	thrown
wear	wore	worn

The idiomatic expressions **used to** and **supposed to** contain regular verbs whose past tense is formed by adding **-d**. Remember to include this ending, even though you may not hear it in spoken English.

Correct the main verbs in the following sentences for past tense and past participle forms. Underline the incorrect verb and write the correction above. If you are uncertain about a form, consult the preceding list of irregular verbs or a dictionary.

1. The women's organization was not use to being ignored by the senator.

2. Before the campers come upon shelter, they almost drownded.

3. There was four children on the playground, and they had come with their teacher.

4. Mona and Fred were suppose to pick up their daughter at 5:30, but their daughter had left because she was use to being picked up at 5:00.

5. The brown dog who had bit the mailman was being protected by the humane society.

6. All of the first graders had drank their daily ration of milk.

7. The worn-out jogger laid on the couch for hours after the race.

8. He use to play soccer in South America before he was recruited by the NFL.

9. Their feet were nearly froze from the hike in subzero weather.

10. The new dress had been wore only three times before the seams gave out.

11. The volleyball team had chose Marsha as the new captain.

12. On Friday, January 18, I received a call from my neighbor's lawyer saying that I'm being sued and was to give a statement to the insurance company.

13. The Atlanta tour had went from Florida to Georgia in record time.

14. The defendant was swore in as a witness while the jury looks on.

15. The sun rose above the Atlantic fog, just as it always has rose.

Proofread the following paragraph making certain that past tense and past participle forms are correct. When you find an incorrect verb form, underline the incorrect verb and write the correction above.

The University basketball team's loss to College at the beginning of the season is the final straw for Coach Brown, and the team knew it. Having been beat mercilessly, the team members at first were embarrassed but later come to realize their faults. When they finally recognized that they pass the ball without accuracy, that they take low percentage shots, and that they lacked team coordination, they vowed to improve their weaknesses. Coach Brown was thankful that the team members came to their senses. The plan for improvement starts with practice. They worked hard. They practice their shooting and passing. During their final games, they learned to play selflessly; they learn that team effort was the best way to win a game.

NAME _____ DATE _____

Starting with one of the phrases or clauses below, write a paragraph of at least five sentences in which you use past tense and past participle forms. If you are uncertain about a form, be sure to consult a dictionary.

1. When I was twelve years old . . .
2. During World War II . . .
3. My father told us that when he was growing up . . .
4. The antiwar rallies of the '60s . . .
5. The first American moon landing . . .
6. Before arriving at the train station . . .
7. In preparation for the tournament . . .
8. At the end of the play . . .
9. After mailing the application . . .
10. From winter to spring . . .

YOUR PARAGRAPH

NAME _____   DATE _____

In the following passage you must fill in the blank with the correct form of the verb in parentheses. Make certain the verb agrees with its subject and that the verb tense is logical and consistent throughout the passage.

When Alice _____ (wake) last Friday morning, she _____ (find) that the snowstorm from the previous night still _____ (rage). The snow _____ (come) down fast and furious and _____ (swirl) big gusts around the houses. The trees _____ (load) with the heavy snow and their branches _____ (strain) under the heavy weight. The utility lines _____ (seem) at the dangerous point of breaking from the freezing temperatures. Outside Alice's house, the cars _____ (park) on the street _____ (have) nearly eighteen inches of snow _____ (pile) atop them.

As Alice _____ (prepare) her breakfast and _____ (ready) herself for work, she _____ (become) concerned about the road and weather conditions. She _____ (turn) on the local radio station and _____ (be) surprised to find out that nearly everyone _____ (close) up their businesses for the day. Of course, schools _____ (close); not even the school buses _____ (leave) the garage because the snowplows _____ (be) unable to _____ (clear) the driveway. The radio station manager _____ (say) nothing about government agencies, however, and Alice _____ (not know) if she _____ (have) to _____ (brave) the elements to _____ (deliver) the mail.

Alice _____ (try) calling her boss at the post office to _____ (see) if she should _____ (go) to work, but she _____ (do not) get through. Her phone _____ (be) out of order; the telephone lines _____ (be) down because of the snow. Now the question _____ (be) whether or not to _____ (attempt) the trip to work. The trip _____ (be) not long, usually a ten-minute drive. But with the snow still _____ (come) down and the streets still _____ (unplow), it _____ (be) treacherous. Alice _____ (decide) that she would _____ (ski) to work rather than _____ (drive) her car. She _____ (gather) together her ski equipment and _____ (check) it to _____ (make) certain she _____ (have) the right wax. After she _____ (change) into her ski togs, she _____ (set off).

The usual ten-minute car trip _____ (turn) into a rather difficult hour-long ski trek. Even though the trip _____ (be) arduous, Alice _____ (think) the scenery _____ (be) beautiful. As she _____ (cross) through the park, the roadways _____ (be) not visible which _____ (make) the area _____ (look) pristine and virginal. And the brightness _____ (be) almost blinding as the snow _____ (glisten) and _____ (sparkle) with an unreal radiance. Crossing over the bridge, Alice _____ (find) small squirrel and rabbit tracks that _____ (lead) into a nearby thicket. Those tracks _____ (be) a sign that the storm _____ (be) past and everyday routines _____ (resume).

When Alice _____ (arrive) at the post office, she _____ (find) her boss just _____ (arrive) in a four-wheel drive jeep. Together they _____ (prepare) the day's mail for the carriers. Then Alice had a hot cup of coffee and the other carriers _____ (join) her as they slowly _____ (make) their ways to the station. As morning _____ (come) to a close, Alice _____ (be) glad she _____ (go) to work. The exercise _____ (prepare) her for her upcoming ski race and the Winter Wonderland scenery _____ (give) her peace of mind.

Grammar

USE OF APOSTROPHE FOR POSSESSIVES AND CONTRACTIONS

Apostrophes, when they identify possessives, help to determine a writer's meaning. Placement of possessive apostrophes becomes particularly important when there are a number of items possessed. Note the following examples:

Bill and Julie's calf, a Jersey, was awarded the blue ribbon at the 4-H competition.

Bill's and Julie's calves, both Herefords, were awarded blue ribbons in the 4-H competition.

These two examples show the number of animals awarded prizes. In the first, we see that Bill and Julie jointly were awarded a prize for their cooperative efforts in showing the Jersey calf. In the second example, Bill and Julie each won an award for their individually shown calves. Other cues which identify the number of animals are the number of the subjects and the subject-verb agreements.

You can see that a misplaced or omitted apostrophe can change the reading of a sentence. Another problem for readers occurs when **its** (the possessive form of the pronoun **it**) and **it's** (the contraction of **it is**) are misused. For example, the two words are misused in the following sentences:

It's collar was lost. (should be **its**, that is, the dog's collar)

Its a collar that was lost. (should be **it's** here, the contraction **it is**)

Note the following rules for forming possessives and contractions.

1   Use of apostrophe for the possessive case of a noun

A. Most common English nouns form the possessive case by adding **'s** (singular) or **s'** (plural). Study the following sentences and note the possessive forms.

The **boy's** ball rolled into the street. (sing.)
The three **boys'** mothers called them to dinner. (pl.)

The squirrel ran away with the **dog's** bone. (sing.)
The **dogs'** leashes were left behind. (pl.)

The **teacher's** desk was cluttered. (sing.)
The **teachers'** meeting lasted two hours. (pl.)

B. The plural forms of some English nouns are **not** formed by adding **s**. These nouns form their plural possessive by adding **'s**.

The **man's** coat was stolen. (sing.)
The **men's** softball game was postponed. (pl.)

The **child's** toy was hidden. (sing.)
The **children's** bikes were locked. (pl.)

The **deer's** fawn rested in the shade. (sing.)
The **deer's** forage area was destroyed. (pl.)

C. Nouns ending in **s** can be made possessive two ways, either of which is correct: The usual way of adding **'s** (Francis's car, the boss's order), or by simply adding **'** (Francis' car, the boss' order).

Francis's car was destroyed in the wreck.
Francis' car was destroyed in the wreck.

The boss's order was carried out fully.
The boss' order was carried out fully.

D. Apostrophes are also used with abstract terms to show possession or to attribute characteristics to those abstractions.

psychology's significance
day's end
hurricane's force
movie's critic
month's salary

NAME _____ DATE _____

Change the first words, as indicated in parentheses, to show singular or plural possession. If you are uncertain about a plural form, use a dictionary.

Example: man (pl.) The **men's** club held its annual meeting.
              cat (sing.) The dog ate the **cat's** food.

1. moth (sing.) The _____ wings fluttered incessantly.

2. month (pl.) He asked for six _____ pay in advance.

3. citizen (pl.) The _____ votes were not counted.

4. team (sing.) His _____ clubhouse has been rebuilt.

5. deer (pl.) The hunters carefully tracked through the forest to the _____ hiding spots.

6. ox (pl.) The _____ yoke was left in the field.

7. Bess (sing.) _____ dress was torn by branches as she ran through the brush.

8. girl (pl.) The _____ soccer team was out of training.

9. man (pl.) The _____ annual golf tournament was rained out.

10. woman (pl.) The new bill was voted down by the _____ action group against sex discrimination.

11. philosophy (sing.) The history professor outlined the _____ importance.

12. code (pl.) The new _____ requirements met stiff opposition from union workers.

13. watcher (pl.), station (sing.) The faulty reception provoked the television _____ anger and prompted them to call the _____ manager.

14. restaurant (sing.) The _____ decor was praised for its tasteful rendering of ancient Rome.

15. marathoner (pl.) All _____ hopes rest on being mentally prepared to finish the race.

24

2 Individual or Joint Possession

Groups of nouns can show individual or joint possession. Pairs of nouns can show individual or joint possession. For example,

John and Mary's mother was a teacher. (one mother, jointly possessed)
John's and **Mary's** mothers are teachers. (two mothers, individually possessed)

The **men and women's** rugby team was controversial. (a rugby team on which both men and women perform)

The **men's** and **women's** locker rooms were clean. (two locker rooms, one for men and one for women)

Group nouns and compound nouns are made possessive by adding **'s**. Their plural possessive is formed by adding **s** to the first word and **'s** to the end of the unit. For example,

The **editor in chief's** decision was final. (sing.)

The **editors in chief's** comments were helpful. (pl.)

The **son-in-law's** car was brand new. (sing.)

The **sons-in-law's** duties were unclear. (pl.)

NAME _____ DATE _____

Change the first words, as indicated in parentheses, to show individual or joint possession, or singular or plural possession. If you are uncertain about plural forms, use a dictionary.

Example: Fred, Lisa (ind.) **Fred's** and **Lisa's** parents were absent.

1. Joe, Jim (joint) _____ mother was ill.

2. Karen, Melissa (ind.) _____ birthdays were on the same day.

3. men, women (ind.) The _____ Olympic trials were postponed.

4. mother-in-law (sing.) The _____ expectations were not easy for the new bride to live up to.

5. Commander in chief (pl.) The _____ final meeting created distrust among them.

6. summer, winter (ind.) The _____ clientele varied greatly at the beach resort.

7. Secretary of State (pl.) The _____ decision was not agreeable to the rulers of the countries.

8. Billy, Francis (joint) The church group met at _____ summer house.

9. passer-by (sing.) The dog nipped at the _____ pant leg.

10. Beth, Maria (ind.) The grand prize was awarded to both _____ apple pies.

11. collector (pl.) Many _____ stamps were placed on display in the foyer.

12. man, woman (ind.) One _____ or one _____ opinion is not enough to convince the jury.

13. Max (sing.) _____ newly organized soccer team was surprisingly well received by the public.

14. editor, reporters (ind.) The _____ and _____ opinions about secrecy of sources did not coincide.

15. manager (pl.) Forty-five advertising firms gathered in Los Angeles to compare their _____ views on computer use.

NAME _____ DATE _____

Change the first words, as indicated in parentheses, to show individual or joint possession, or singular or plural possession. If you are uncertain about plural forms, use a dictionary.

Example: actor (sing.) The **actor's** line was not heard.
man (pl.) The **men's** club held its annual meeting.

1. Paul (sing.) _____ ball rolled into the street.

2. Fred, George (joint) _____ car placed first in the rally.

3. lady-in-waiting (pl.) The _____ flowers were not ready in time for the rehearsal.

4. it (sing.) His rusty, old wagon lay on _____ side.

5. hawk (pl.) They found no eggs in the _____ nests.

6. Keats (sing.) _____ odes have become known as examples of Romantic poetry.

7. Woman (pl.) _____ clothes are constantly changing.

8. ox (sing.) The _____ yoke broke in the middle of plowing.

9. mother-in-law (pl.) Everyone admired the _____ kindness to the new brides.

10. Margaret, Bill (ind.) _____ books were left behind.

11. stock market (sing.) The 1984 _____ gains was remarkable compared to previous years.

12. Smiths, Jones (joint) The _____ and _____ investment in a resort hotel was not as profitable as they hoped.

13. expert (pl.) The nutrition _____ preparation of a special diet plan for people weighing over 300 pounds was commendable.

14. dog (sing.) Evidence of the crime was found in the _____ pen.

15. Francine, Marcie (ind.) _____ and _____ test scores revealed their hard work in preparing for the exam.

3 *its* and *it's*

Mistakes in the use of the apostrophe with the pronoun **it** result from the two **s** forms of the word **it**. **Its** is the possessive case of the pronoun **it**; **it's** is the contraction of **it is** or **it has**. Avoid the mistake of confusing **it's** with the possessive form of **it**, **its**. Note the following examples.

The dog broke **its** leg. (the leg of the dog)

It's a hot, humid day. (It is a hot, humid day.)

4 Contractions combine two words into one.

An apostrophe also indicates that one or more letters have been omitted; this structure is called a contraction. Sometimes contractions are confused with possessives, such as **its** and **it's** mentioned earlier. Beware of the possible confusion that results in misusing **its/it's**, **their/they're**, and **your/you're**. **Its**, **their**, and **your** are possessives; **it's**, **they're**, and **you're** are contractions. Study the following contractions:

I am	I'm
you are	you're
(he, she, it, who) is	he's, she's, it's, who's
(we, they) are	we're, they're
I will	I'll
you will	you'll
they will	they'll
I would	I'd
you would	you'd
they would	they'd

The negatives of **are, is, could, do, does, should,** and **would** are formed by adding the contraction **n't**: **aren't, isn't, couldn't, don't, doesn't, shouldn't, couldn't**. Two exceptions are **will not** (won't) and **cannot** (can't). The negative contraction of **I am** is **I'm not**.

Beware of contractions using **have**. Often you may write what you hear rather than the correct contraction form. For example, **You should have gone** becomes **You should've gone**, not **You should of gone**.

NAME _____ DATE _____

Fill in the blanks to complete the following pattern showing contractions.

		CONTRACTION	NEGATIVE CONTRACTION
Example:	**we will**	**we'll**	**we won't**
1.	_____	she'll	she won't
2.	it is	_____	it isn't
3.	_____	who's	who isn't
4.	I am	I'm	_____
5.	they are	_____	_____
6.	_____	they'd	they won't
7.	_____	_____	it won't
8.	you are	you're	_____
9.	he will	_____	_____
10.	_____	I'd	_____
11.	_____	_____	he isn't
12.	you will	_____	_____
13.	you would	_____	_____
14.	_____	_____	she isn't
15.	we are	_____	we aren't

Grammar

PRONOUNS

1 Pronoun/Antecedent Agreement

A pronoun must agree in number, person, and gender with the word to which it refers. A pronoun is a word that replaces a noun to avoid repetition. The word (noun) to which a pronoun refers is called the antecedent.

A. If a noun is singular, the pronoun must be singular. If a noun is plural, the pronoun must be plural. Note the faults in the following examples and how they've been corrected.

The **secretaries** got **her** wages.

Rewrite:
The **secretaries** got **their** wages. (plural)

or

The **secretary** got **her** wages. (singular)

The new-found **religion** did not reveal **their** truths to just anyone.

Rewrite:
The new-found **religion** did not reveal **its** truths to just anyone. (singular)

Sometimes it's difficult to identify the number of a noun. Be sure to familiarize yourself with the collective nouns that can be singular or plural:

The coach will be happy if Iowa (win, wins) (its, their) first championship.

The inference here is that a team working as a unit accomplished something. So the singular antecedent and verb are used:

The coach will be happy if Iowa wins its first championship.

B. Also a pronoun must agree in person with its antecedent. If a noun is first, second, or third person, the pronoun must reflect that person. Study the following examples:

	SINGULAR	PLURAL
1st person	I	we
2nd person	you	you
3rd person	he, she, it	they

My mother said **he** should mind **my** own business.

Rewrite:
My mother said **I** should mind **my** own business.

Our family does own that land. **You** have owned it for fifty years.

Rewrite:
Our family does own that land. **We** have owned it for fifty years. (first person, plural)

C. A pronoun must agree with its antecedent in gender. If a noun is feminine, masculine, or neuter, the pronoun must reflect that gender. Note the following example:

The **billing** was not in **his** proper form.

Rewrite:
The **billing** was not in **its** proper form.

Sexism in pronoun use has become a sticky problem in recent years. The she/he or s/he or him/her notations have tried to accommodate this troublesome area; however, they often create awkward expressions. If you know the gender of a noun, then use the proper antecedent.

The manager left her office at 3:00 P.M.

The swimmer pulled his leg muscle.

There are situations where you might not be able to identify the gender of a noun. For example, occupational and professional titles do not indicate masculinity or femininity. If you are uncertain of a noun's gender, using the plural form or eliminating the antecedent can reduce the problem.

The doctor makes (his or her?) rounds every day.

Rewrite:
The doctor makes rounds every day.

or

The doctors make their rounds every day.

NAME _____ DATE _____

Underline the pronoun form in parentheses that would be preferred and indicate the pronoun's person and number. If necessary, change the sentence to avoid awkward constructions.

Example: One must keep (<u>himself</u>, themselves) fit with a healthy diet. **3rd person, singular**

1. A person has to run (her, their) own life. _____

2. The baby was found by (its, his) mother. _____

3. Captain Kangaroo asked Mr. Greenjeans if (they, he) found the rabbit.

   _____

4. After Michigan won the title, (they, it) went to play in the Rose Bowl.

   _____

5. Neither of them will give (their, her) sanction to the project. _____

6. Each of the boys ran as fast as (he, they) could. _____

7. Everyone must watch (his, their) own hot dog. _____

8. One must work at least twenty years before (he, they) can be eligible for a pension.

   _____

9. The committee (has, have) always voted according to (their, its) wives' say-so.

   _____

10. Each girl must make certain (they, she) is on time. _____

NAME _____ DATE _____

Substitute pronouns for the repeated nouns in the second sentence. The pronouns should reflect the proper number, person, and gender of their antecedents.

Example: My sister asked Ron not to bring the dog.
              She   it
        ~~My sister~~ said that ~~the dog~~ would disrupt the party.

1. Dave gave Dora a new dress for a Christmas present.

Dave thought Dora would like a new dress.

2. The governor's son went to a used-car dealer and bought a motorcycle.

The motorcycle didn't cost the governor's son too much, but the motorcycle

makes a lot of noise.

3. All the players on the basketball team have suffered injured knees this year.

It makes one wonder why the players keep on playing.

4. Last night there was a TV special about a whale.

The TV special showed people how the whale breathes.

5. Those children down the street are always picking on my dog.

Last week the dog really got even with those children.

6. Everybody knows about those sales because the weekly flyer had a special

advertisement.

However, the sales were not what the flyer said they would be.

7. My baby brother spilled orange juice all over Mother's new rug.

When Mother returned home, she was furious with baby brother.

8. While strolling through the woods, Fred spotted a mother bear and her cubs.

Fred was not frightened when the mother bear charged.

9. The doctors contribute overtime to the new clinic.

The clinic does not pay the doctors.

10. Barbara teaches creative writing every Wednesday evening.

At that time Barbara spends fifteen minutes with each student.

11. The couple played tennis twice a week.

The couple's wins were even.

12. Pies and cakes were the attraction at the bakery booth.

Many people bought pies and cakes.

13. Working in the mines exhausted Fred's energy.

Fred's exhaustion caused a vitamin deficiency.

14. France makes superb champagne.

Many wine connoisseurs will drink only champagne.

15. The computers were destroyed by the fire.

The computers will be replaced by newer models.

2 Special Pronoun Structures

There are some troublesome pronoun structures which need careful attention. Make certain that the antecedent is clear or else you may end up confusing your reader.

A. When two or more antecedents are joined by **and**, the pronoun is plural. Note the following examples:

Janice and I went to the dress shop, and then **we** had a soda.

If **Nancy and John** are lucky, **they** will beat **their** previous records.

B. When the antecedent is a collective noun, the pronoun may be singular or plural depending on whether the noun is considered as a unit or individuals acting on their own. Note examples:

The **team** was not playing **its** best. (singular)

The **team** voted for **their** new captains. (plural)

C. **Everyone, everybody, anybody, anyone,** and **each** take singular verbs and should be referred to by a singular pronoun. (See p. 7 and pp. 30–31)

    Everyone needs **their** toothbrush.

Rewrite:
    Everyone needs **his or her** toothbrush.

D. **All, some,** and **none** are singular or plural depending on the context. The prepositional phrase following the noun specifies whether it is singular or plural. Note the example:

Some of the fabric lost **its** coloring. (singular)

Some of the young men turned in **their** draft cards. (plural)

E. **This** and **that** are demonstrative pronouns which refer to a whole idea in a previous sentence rather than a particular object or person in that sentence. You must be cautious in using **this** or **that** in order for the reader to understand your reference. If **this** or **that** refers to a complex or complicated notion, it might be better to use **this** or **that** as a demonstrative adjective followed by a noun which summarizes the sentence's main idea. For example:

Acceptable: I enjoyed the mountains, but **this** revealed to me that I really prefer a vacation at the beach.

Better: I enjoyed the mountains, but **this experience** revealed to me that I really prefer a vacation at the beach.

NAME _____ DATE _____

Choose the correct pronoun in parentheses and underline it.

Example: Jane wanted to find out if the students passed (his, <u>their</u>) tests.

1. Don't you think salesclerks should be more courteous to (their, its) customers?

2. Studying grammar may help students improve (them, their) writing.

3. Try to ignore Pat and Tom; (they, them) are just trying to gain attention.

4. Doing daily exercises is not fun for lots of people; (she, they) would rather drink coffee.

5. The tennis team won their matches and (those, those victories) made (it, them) happy.

6. Anybody who wants to come along should get (their, his) jacket.

7. Some of the paint dried up in (its, their) can.

8. The family went to the church of (its, their) choice.

9. I would like to have a million dollars, but (that, that wealth) would make me frivolous.

10. Each of the new students should have (their, his or her) enrollment card.

11. The fundraiser's staff was commended for (their, its) success.

12. The various prescriptions were mailed to (their, its) respective patients.

13. The boys' baseball team was overwhelmed by (its, their) annual statistics.

14. Each member of the library staff has (their, his or her) specific duty.

15. The newly landscaped park and (their, its) new bicycle trails was a great asset to the region.

NAME _____ DATE _____

Write the correct pronoun in the blank and underline its antecedent.

Example: <u>Mary</u> passed the biology test because <u>she</u> studied.

1. George and Lisa are planning a trip to British Columbia as soon as _____ save enough money.

2. Four students were running the university bookstore when the president dismissed _____ for incompetence.

3. Joe has a class schedule that interferes with _____ work schedule.

4. Don't you think all of the students need _____ own utensils?

5. The newspaper was discredited for abuse of the incumbent candidate, but _____ campaign was not affected.

6. The President seems to feel that _____ proposal will be accepted by the senators.

7. Whenever Father arrives late, Mother really gives _____ a piece of _____ mind.

8. Four new tenants had _____ apartments burglarized.

9. What if no one reads the advertisement? Then _____ won't shop at the new boutique.

10. Everyone said to Linda that _____ was a ravishing beauty.

11. Fifteen of the twenty managers requested that _____ offices be moved.

12. The loan officers might have told the tellers that _____ would have to comply with the new dress code.

13. The journal's new format pleased _____ continuing readership.

14. Alice's expectations for _____ children were difficult for _____ to accomplish.

15. These old blankets have outlived _____ usefulness.

NAME _____ DATE _____

In the following sentences write the correct pronoun in the blank.

Example: Doug and Karen were hoping that **they** could meet the train on time.

1. The young boy and his dog started on _____ trip around the world.

2. The price of potatoes is not what _____ used to be.

3. The choir could not perform _____ Sunday best because of too many illnesses.

4. If the town sheriff is re-elected, _____ says _____ will stop dogs from barking.

5. My mother says that _____ cannot buy that new formal that I want.

6. The palm reader said, "_____ should watch your wrist lines carefully.

   _____ will tell _____ future."

7. Harriet could not find _____ new brooch.

8. The master marksman could hit any target with _____ special pistol.

9. All of the babies were waiting to see _____ doctors.

10. Everyone needs to find _____ niche in the world.

11. Anyone who is not in bed in ten minutes will not get _____ dessert tomorrow.

12. You must find _____ jacket before boarding the train.

13. The booster club met for _____ weekly pep session.

14. Mark and I will come directly after _____ finish cleaning the car.

15. The maps do not indicate that city. How will Bob and Terry find _____

way?

16. How is the mistress of ceremonies going to introduce _____ husband?

17. In South America, the people do a lot of handiwork so _____ can sell

_____ to tourists.

18. Each of the dominoes should be placed with _____ dotted side facing up.

19. The camera that Bertha bought is not the one _____ wanted.

20. The circus drove into town with all _____ animals leashed behind

_____ biggest van.

21. Are you unable to pursue _____ education?

22. Your children's new school has had _____ playground renovated.

23. Mail carriers have found _____ jobs interesting.

24. Each of the brothers was warned about _____ tardiness.

25. Theater-goers were waiting for _____ tickets.

After reading the following passage, fill in the blanks with the appropriate pronouns.

Bob and Carol were very fond of Trixie, a dog _____ had for nearly

ten years. _____ took _____ dog on every summer vacation, usually

to Vermont, and to Thanksgiving and Christmas dinners in Ohio; Trixie

went everywhere _____ went. _____ was well behaved and

adjusted to new settings as long as _____ owners were around. At

home, Trixie followed Carol and Bob everywhere and was very

protective of _____.

All of _____ neighbors were fond of Trixie, especially the children.

Often _____ would ask to play with Trixie or to take _____ for

walks. Carol and Bob were always glad to have Trixie so well attended

and gladly let the children play with _____. Once Trixie even saved

one of the children from a terrible accident. Little Tommy Smith was

walking Trixie around the block when a pickup truck, traveling much

too fast, nearly hit Tommy. If Trixie hadn't pushed _____ out of the

truck's path, Tommy would have been injured.

Yes, Trixie was a lifesaver; another time _____ saved Bob and

Carol from a terrible fate. One evening as _____ were settling into

bed, Trixie, who usually beds down at the same time, became very alert

and anxious. _____ whinings and excited behavior should have

warned Bob and Carol that _____ might be in danger but _____

paid no attention; _____ just went to sleep as usual. Because Trixie

was so small, _____ was hard for _____ to get _____ masters'

attention once _____ were asleep. Trixie's only resort was barking and

then _____ just got a slipper thrown at _____. Finally after frantic efforts, Trixie took a giant leap onto the middle of the bed, a phenomenal feat for _____ size. _____ woke Bob and Carol and _____ found _____ in the midst of a smoke-filled room.

Apparently the fire _____ had built in the fireplace accidentally ignited the woodpile nearby. The fire was a long time smoldering before _____ became dangerous. _____ was Trixie who saved Bob and Carol. Once _____ all were safe, Bob and Carol showered Trixie with _____ thanks. Because of _____ persistent warnings, _____ masters were safe and _____ house sustained very little damage.

Grammar

ITEM 25

DANGLING VERBALS

An introductory verbal or verbal phrase must have its "doer" in the subject of the main clause. If the verbal is not attached to the proper agent, it is a **dangling** verbal. You should make certain that the subject of the main clause is the "doer" of the action specified in the preceding verbal phrase. Note the faults in the following examples and the way they have been corrected.

> VERBAL PHRASE   SUBJECT
> **Running through the woods, George's shoes** were lost.

Rewrite:

> VERBAL PHRASE   SUBJECT
> **Running through the woods, George** lost his shoes.

> VERBAL PHRASE   SUBJECT
> **To accomplish this end, studying** grammar and usage is necessary.

Rewrite:

> VERBAL PHRASE   SUBJECT
> **To accomplish this end, we** must study grammar and usage.

> VERBAL PHRASE   SUBJECT
> **Floating in her lemonade, Mary** found a fly.

Rewrite:

> SUBJECT   VERBAL PHRASE
> **Mary** found a fly **floating in her lemonade.**

Correct the following sentences, which have dangling verbals, by rearranging the main clause in such a way that the subject of the clause will be the "doer" of the action indicated in the introductory verbal phrase.

Example: To take off, the plane's engine was started by John.
              To take off, John started the plane's engine.

1. Shining brightly, Francis watched the moon.

2. To win the race, it was necessary for Juan to run faster than ever.

3. By rowing to the island, the mail could be picked up by Mary and Jack.

4. Walking to the top of the stairs, the alarm was tripped by Bill.

5. To bake the cake, butter and eggs were needed by Kay.

6. In developing the film, certain chemicals were needed by the printer.

7. In memory of the veterans, the tree was planted by the club.

8. When finding the courts crowded, the tennis team's patience was lost.

9. Weeding the five-mile radius, the garden was cleared by the prisoners.

10. Following her brother, the way home was discovered by Marian.

NAME _____ DATE _____

Some of the following sentences use verbal phrases correctly; place a *C* next to them. Correct those sentences that have dangling verbals by rearranging the main clause in such a way that the subject of the clause will be the "doer" of the action indicated in the introductory phrase.

1. After falling head over heels in love, marriage was Tom and Ann's next step.

2. In looking for new shoes, Mary discovered how high prices were.

3. To accommodate the convention, extra rooms were reserved by the hotel manager.

4. Chopping the fire wood, it was necessary for Tim to split logs.

5. While training for the marathon, running ten miles was Andrea's daily goal.

6. In eating strawberries and shortcake, the juice ran over Ted's new shirt.

7. Discovering the new trail, the mountain became a new interest for the local residents.

8. In order to start the mower, the handle needs to be depressed by the operator.

9. To correct an error in judgment, the new road plan was proposed by the race judges.

10. In order to pick up a friend at the airport, Jim had to meet a 5:00 A.M. plane.

Complete the following sentences by combining (a) the main clauses and (b) the verbal phrases. It may be necessary to reword the main clauses in order to clearly identify the "doer" of the verbal phrase's action.

Example:　a. the police were called by Dorothy.
　　　　　　b. after hearing the scream

　　　　　Dorothy called the police after hearing the scream.

1. a. it was necessary for Dennis to view the line-up
　 b. to identify the criminal

2. a. the police received a call from the kidnappers
　 b. threatening the hostage's life

3. a. the bear frightened the Girl Scouts
　 b. shouting for help

4. a. the gospel was sung by the choir
　 b. envisioning the splendor of heaven

5. a. the opportunity to embezzle funds was taken by Mr. Jones
　 b. while managing the Hotel Lorraine

6. a. the pills were miscounted by the pharmacist
　 b. while filling the prescription

7. a. the local address had to be maintained by Ron for six months
   b. to establish residency

8. a. the police officer was not relieved on time
   b. forgotten by the new recruit

9. a. the whistle was blown by the engineer
   b. before arriving at the train station

10. a. John heard the autumn wind
   b. blowing through the pine trees

Grammar

MISPLACED MODIFIERS

Misplaced modifiers can lead to a misreading of a sentence. If a word or phrase or clause is not placed as closely as possible to the words it modifies, the reader can become confused and misinterpret your idea. A sentence or part of a sentence can be ambiguous if modifiers are put in the wrong places. You must take care to place modifiers in their proper places or to revise cluttered sentences in order to make ideas and their modifiers clear.

---

1 Words that are modifiers can be misplaced and create confusion.

Consider this sentence:

The people who saw the TV series frequently praised it.

The difficulty here is that the word **frequently** comes between **saw the TV series** and **praised it**; the word **frequently** could modify either of these phrases. This sentence could be reworded as follows:

The people who frequently saw the TV series praised it.
(**Frequently** in this position must apply to **saw**.)

The people who saw the TV series praised it frequently.
(In this position, **frequently** must apply to **praised**.)

Consider this second example:

The zoo keepers captured the escaped gorilla carefully returning it to its cage.

The difficulty here is similar to the previous example. The adverb **carefully** comes between **captured the escaped gorilla** and **returning it to its cage** and could modify either phrase. The sentence may be revised as follows:

The zoo keepers **carefully** captured the escaped gorilla, returning it to its cage.

or

The zoo keepers captured the escaped gorilla, **carefully** returning it to its cage.

or

The zoo keepers captured the escaped gorilla, returning it **carefully** to its cage.

2 Phrases and clauses can be misplaced and create confusion.

Consider this sentence:

I saw the girl in the car that moved.

Was it the girl that moved or the car that moved? **That moved** is unclear because **that** can refer to both people and things. The following revisions, however, are clear:

I saw the girl in the car who moved.

or

I saw the girl who moved in the car.

Either sentence is clearer because **who** can refer only to people, not things.

or

I saw the girl in the car which moved.

Here, the *car* moved because **which** refers only to things.

3 **Sometimes a greater change in structure is required to clarify a modification. Some changes may correct other faults in addition to ambiguity.**

The following sentence is not only ambiguous but also wordy:

He took the book in the car that was blue.

In this sentence you can assume that **that is blue** modifies **car** because of its position. However, since **that** refers to things, there is a possibility of the clause modifying **book** as well. Either meaning may be expressed clearly in a simpler sentence.

He took the blue book in the car.

or

He took the book in the blue car.

NAME _____ DATE _____

Each of the following sentences contains an underlined phrase that is misplaced. Rewrite the sentences, placing the phrases so that they modify the material indicated in parentheses.

Example: The children were so hungry that they <u>almost</u> ate all the cookies. (to modify <u>cookies</u>)

The children were so hungry that they ate <u>almost</u> all the cookies.

1. The general showed how battles are often lost <u>in a series of lectures</u>. (to modify <u>showed</u>)

2. She had two large albums showing pictures of her family <u>hidden in the basement</u>. (to modify <u>albums</u>)

3. I chose the black horse for my sister <u>with the good temper</u>. (to modify <u>black horse</u>)

4. There was one course that showed students how to set off crude bombs <u>at the university</u>. (to modify <u>course</u>)

5. The old man found a green toad <u>searching in the grass for his glasses</u>. (to modify <u>the old man</u>)

6. We saw the child with the bag of candy <u>that was attractive</u>. (to modify <u>the child</u>)

7. She spoke to the boy <u>with a warm smile</u>. (to modify <u>She</u>)

8. She decided to send the shirts to the cleaners <u>that were dirty</u>. (to modify <u>shirts</u>)

9. The garden was cleared by the boy scout troop <u>which was overgrown with weeds</u>. (to modify <u>garden</u>)

10. He arrived accompanied by a German shepherd <u>with a big smile on his face</u>. (to modify <u>He</u>)

11. There were four children <u>only</u> riding the bus. (to modify <u>four children</u>)

12. Brad and Tim were frightened <u>suddenly</u> glancing into the cave. (to modify <u>frightened</u>)

13. The citrus growers complained about the weather <u>with a bitter vengeance</u>. (to modify <u>complained</u>)

14. The new homes were built by the contractors <u>along the Old Mill Road</u>. (to modify <u>homes</u>)

15. Readers paid huge sums to finance the manuscripts showings <u>that were interested</u>. (to modify <u>readers</u>)

NAME _____ DATE _____

Each of the following sentences contains a word or phrase that is misplaced. Rewrite the sentences in order to place the modifier in a position that answers the question following the sentence.

1. Magazines are read by adults that have dirty words. (What has dirty words?)

2. The sixth graders watched patiently waiting for the principal. (How did the students wait?)

3. Martin met Stan in the hallway looking for his misplaced cap. (What was Stan doing in the hallway?)

4. While she was cleaning the stove, the kitten ran past the maid. (What was the maid doing?)

5. The woods were full of critters with deep, dark shadows. (What had deep, dark shadows?)

6. Martha sifted the flour carefully preparing the apple pie. (How did Martha sift flour?)

7. The greenhouses attracted giant spiders which were transparent. (What was transparent?)

8. The father rocked the baby gently singing him to sleep. (How did the father rock?)

9. The policemen caught the young criminals who ran past the grocery. (Which policemen?)

10. The split pea soup tasted good to the lady in the black pot. (Where was the soup?)

11. College prepares students for a career while still working. (What do students do in college?)

12. She only had left a pair of slippers. (What if she owns one pair of slippers?)

13. George gave the book of Shakespeare's plays to Marilyn from the library. (Where is the book from?)

14. The doctor prescribed aspirin for the patient in the white coat. (What is the doctor wearing?)

15. The kitten was chased by the dog that was black and white. (What color is the kitten?)

NAME _____ DATE _____

**Remember that modifiers should be placed close to the words
they modify. Complete the following sentences by placing the
italicized phrases in positions that point clearly to what they
modify. State the writer's meaning in parentheses following
the sentences. If necessary, rewrite the sentences.**

Example: *which were delicacies*

The mushrooms _____ were mixed with the carrots
_____.

(to modify *mushrooms*)
The mushrooms **which were delicacies** were mixed with the carrots.

1. *who was sitting on the bench*

The daughter _____ was waiting for her mother

_____.

(   )

2. *wearing a green button*

Each new salesman _____ sold a used car _____.

(   )

3. *waiting in the rain*

The students _____ finally boarded the school bus

_____.

(   )

4. *in Milan, Michigan*

Fathers and sons _____ cheered at the banquet _____.

(   )

5. *carrying bread crumbs*

The ants _____ crawled over the man _____.

(   )

6. *with four apple pies*

Jane and Fred _____ went _____ to the county fair

_____.

(   )

7. *who were underpaid*

In 1983, the workers _____ gathered in protest with their supervisors

_____.

(   )

8. *who thought there would be a tip*

The young waitress _____ helped the salesman _____.

(   )

9. *with a real estate broker*

The Smiths found _____ their new home _____.

(   )

10. *which usually stayed in the barn*

The birds _____ chirped in the trees _____.

(   )

Grammar

PARALLELISM

You should preserve parallel structure by using units of the same grammatical kind in pairs or a series of items. The principle governing parallelism is that a pair or series of coordinate units should be of the same kind—nouns with nouns, adjectives with adjectives, phrases with phrases, clauses with clauses, and so on—not a mixture of nouns and phrases. A breakdown in parallelism destroys coherence because it disrupts the reader's expectation started by a series beginning with one kind of unit. Parallelism can also eliminate wordy repetitions and can clarify logical relations among cases.

1 Parallel Words

When a parallel structure involves single words, make certain they are of the same grammatical kind. Note the faults in the following sentences and how they are corrected.

NOUN   ADJECTIVE

The old beliefs about theft have been rejected as **superstitions** and **detrimental**.

Rewrite:

ADJECTIVE   ADJECTIVE

The old beliefs about theft have been rejected as **superstitious** and **detrimental**.

NOUN   NOUN   ADJECTIVE

He was a **miser,** a **bachelor,** and **egotistical.**

Rewrite:

NOUN   NOUN   NOUN

He was a **miser,** a **bachelor,** and an **egotist.**

or

ADJECTIVE   ADJECTIVE   ADJECTIVE

He was **miserly, unmarried,** and **egotistical.**

---

2   Parallel Phrases

The same principle applies to the use of phrases within a sentence. The phrases should be of the same kind—prepositional phrases with prepositional phrases, infinitive phrases with infinitive phrases—not infinitive phrases with prepositional phrases.

The professor enjoyed teaching English literature to the students
INFINITIVE PHRASE   PREPOSITIONAL PHRASE
to enhance their education and **for their enjoyment.**

Rewrite:
The professor enjoyed teaching English literature to the students
PREPOSITIONAL PHRASE   PREPOSITIONAL PHRASE
for the enhancement of their education and **for their enjoyment.**

or

The professor enjoyed teaching English literature to the students
INFINITIVE PHRASE   INFINITIVE PHRASE
to enhance their education and **to entertain them.**

---

3   Parallel Clauses

Again, the parallel principle applies to pairs of clauses. Most often an error in this category is made when clauses and phrases are mixed. Note the following example:

PREPOSITIONAL PHRASE

The President commended the steelworkers **for their patriotism** and
ADVERB CLAUSE

because they did not ask for a wage increase.

Rewrite:

The President commended the steelworkers **because they were patriotic** and **because they did not ask for a wage increase.**

or

The President commended the steelworkers **for being patriotic** and **for refraining from asking for a wage increase.**

The parallel principle also applies to the use of independent clauses and sentences. With the use of correlative conjunctions (**either . . . or; neither . . . nor; not only . . . but also**), grammatical structures must be the same on the right side of both conjunctions.

The advertisers not only **convince the reader that the Continental is a luxury car** but also **that the car confers status on its owner.**

Rewrite:

The advertisers not only **convince the reader that the Continental is a luxury car** but also **convince the reader that the car confers status on its owner.**

or

Advertisers convince the reader not only **that the Continental is a luxury car** but also **that the car confers status on its owner.**

You will notice that the above rewrites are more emphatic and clearer when parallel structures are used. Also note that the rewrites are balanced; the parallel clauses are nearly the same length and have similar rhythm.

Parallel use of independent clauses and sentences can be particularly useful when you want to highlight a contrast; this is called an antithetical sentence. Note how the following example has been rewritten to emphasize a contrast.

You may purchase an inexpensive house but the mortgage loan will have high interest rates.

Rewrite:

You may purchase an inexpensive house but you may pay high interest on a mortgage loan.

NAME _____ DATE _____

Rewrite each of the following sentences so as to fulfill the reader's expectations of parallel structure. Also indicate the original inconsistency by labeling the grammatical parts in the series. You may have to change the wording to create coherence and balance.

                         NOUN   PREPOSITIONAL PHRASES

Example: Mary went **grocery shopping, to the bank,** and **into the car wash.**
            Mary went to the grocery, to the bank, and to the car wash.

1. The tennis players were held over in Chicago and staying overnight.

2. The librarians tried everything to improve their facility: longer hours, allowing food, they even improved the lighting.

3. The soccer team either is making an extraordinary number of points, or the fans think they look good.

4. Keats' poems are passionate, insightful, and works of beauty.

5. The new office manager was kinder, more fun, with better humor and more tact.

6. The seven young students marched on the president's office demanding more liberal arts courses and asked for a new library.

7. The troops were rewarded for their outstanding performance and because they were brave.

8. The police officers rushed to the accident but the crowd was already out of hand.

9. The new humanities course was offered during the fall semester and being taught by the English and Foreign Language departments.

10. When Maria stepped from the boat she saw the city of Buenos Aires with its people, scents, sounds, and incredibly confusing.

11. The morning after the race, Jill felt tired, was injured, and wanted to eat.

12. The ice fishers broke the ice and a shelter was erected.

13. The company workers were under investigation for fraud and because they were striking.

14. The baseball team's pitcher was on a temporary contract but it would allow an extension.

15. The annual fundraiser for the orphans was postponed because there was a lack of interest and no one would host the benefit.

Examine the following paragraphs and point out the types of parallel structures. Briefly discuss their effectiveness.

1. Poetry turns all things to loveliness; it exalts the beauty of that which is most beautiful and it adds beauty to that which is most deformed; it marries exaltation and horror, grief and pleasure, eternity and change; it subdues to union under its light yoke, all irreconcilable things. It transmutes all that it touches, and every form moving within the radiance of its presence is changed by wondrous sympathy to an incarnation of the spirit which it breathes; its secret alchemy turns potable gold the poisonous waters which flow from death through life; it strips the veil of familiarity from the world, and lays bare the naked and sleeping beauty which is the spirit of its form.

    (Percy Bysshe Shelley, 1821)

2. These are the times that try men's souls: the summer soldier and the sunshine patriot will in this crisis, shrink from the service of his country; but he that stands it NOW, deserves the love and thanks of man and woman. Tyranny, like hell, is not easily conquered; yet we have this consolation with us, that the harder the conflict, the more glorious the triumph. What we obtain too cheap, we esteem too lightly.

    (Thomas Paine, 1776)

3. Evermore it is the order of nature to grow, and every soul is by this intrinsic necessity quitting its whole system of things, its friends and home and laws and faith, as the shell fish crawls out of its beautiful but stony case, because it no longer admits of its growth, and slowly forms a new house.

    (Ralph Waldo Emerson, 1841)

NAME _____ DATE _____

Follow the instructions in these items to create sentences with parallel structures. You may have to change the word forms to achieve the requested parallels.

1. *drink, fall, swim*
   Write two sentences, one using the present tense of these verbs and another using the verbs in participial phrases.

2. *tired, frustrated, angry*
   Write two sentences, one using these words as adjectives, the other using them as nouns.

3. *morning, noon, night*
   Use these words as adjectives in one sentence and in prepositional phrases in another sentence.

4. *song, dance, performance*
   Write two sentences, one using these words as nouns, the other using them as verbs.

5. *gather, recover, restore*
   Use these words as main verbs in one sentence and in phrases in another sentence.

The following passage has many problems with misplaced modifiers, dangling verbals, and faulty parallelism. Revise this passage making it more direct and concise by eliminating the troublesome structures.

The backpacking trip to the Northwest had been planned since May and the Edwards family was looking forward to this venture with anticipation. To prepare for this trip in the Bitteroot Mountains of Montana and Idaho, the Forest Service was contacted and requested maps and they also asked for advice from the rangers. By consulting outdoor guides and they talked to recreation experts, they carefully selected the necessary equipment and planned the route of the hike.

Since the trip was coordinated by all of the family, each person was responsible for some part of the preparation. Together, they felt they had enough experience and expertise to make the trip pleasant and enjoyable, and it would be successful. Because Joseph had traveled to this Montana area before he knew the equipment that was necessary. So his task was to put together all the packs, sleeping bags, tents, there was a cook stove and some tools. Being a nurse, the first aid kit was Dorothy's responsibility. She would also brush up on first aid skills for the wilderness by familiarizing herself with snakes and plants poisonous to the area. Having participated in numerous long hikes, their son, Bill, was familiar with various quickly prepared foods that were highly nutritious too. He was going to gather the food supply paying careful attention to optimum nutrition and checking minimal weight. Gathering all the maps for the main routes, water holes were located by Janet, their daughter. She would make sure of alternate routes for emergencies with notes on required hiking skills. All this preparation was to assure a trouble-free trip; the Edwards knew the importance of being prepared.

Over the few weeks preceding their trip, the Edwards began packing and· rechecked the weight of each pack. Everything was taken into consideration, from cook stoves and tools to toiletries and they even checked the pencils and paper. Trying to get into shape for the hike, individual exercise programs were developed for each family member. They had daily routines to build up stamina and strength. By the time they were ready to leave on the trip, all the necessities were in perfect order and Joseph, Dorothy, Bill and Janet were in excellent physical condition. They felt they were prepared for anything that would happen.

Grammar

ITEM 29

SENTENCE FRAGMENTS

---

1 Common types of fragments

A sentence or independent clause is a complete thought which has a subject and a predicate with a verb as its main grammatical elements. Although a dependent clause has a subject and verb, it does not present a complete thought; a dependent clause's meaning is made dependent (subordinate) by the subordinating conjunction or relative pronoun at the head of the string. Thus, a dependent clause does not present a complete thought because its whole idea is dependent on another, independent clause.

A sentence fragment is commonly defined as a string of words, between an initial capital letter and a period or question mark, that lacks a subject or verb predicate or both. But a sentence fragment also occurs when a dependent clause is passed off as a complete thought. Remember that a dependent clause is not a complete thought even though it may have a subject and verb. A dependent clause cannot stand by itself as a complete thought; it is a fragment.

Following are some examples of fragments and ways to correct them. In the rewrites, you will notice a number of ways to correct sentence fragments by linking them with independent clauses. This is done by eliminating the unnecessary end punctuation and supplying the proper internal punctuation and/or coordinating/subordinating words. Remember that there is no one way to correct a fragment. Choose the method which best suits the purpose and style of your writing assignment.

Common Types of Fragments

1. NOUN CLAUSE AS APPOSITIVE:
The only type of administrators we want are honest ones. **People who tell the truth.** (lacks a predicate)

Rewrite:
The only type of administrators we want are honest ones, people who will tell the truth.

or

The only type of administrators we want are honest people who will tell the truth.

2. PREPOSITIONAL PHRASE:
Bill tried to climb Mt. Everest, but it was too difficult. **With the winter snow and ice.** (lacks subject and predicate)

Rewrite:
Bill tried to climb Mt. Everest, but it was too difficult with the winter snow and ice.

or

The winter snow and ice made it too difficult for Bill to climb Mt. Everest.

3. PARTICIPLE PHRASE:
The concert was exciting because of the rock group. **Running around, jumping off stage, and playing their instruments loudly.** (lacks subject and predicate)

Rewrite:
The concert was exciting because of the rock group running around, jumping off stage, and playing their instruments loudly.

or

The rock group's running around, jumping off stage, and playing their instruments loudly made the concert exciting.

4. INFINITIVE PHRASE:
After the semester was over, I had only one thought. **To go to the beach and bask in the sun.** (lacks subject and predicate)

Rewrite:
After the semester was over, I had only one thought: to go to the beach and bask in the sun.

or

After the semester was over, I had only one thought—to go to the beach and bask in the sun.

5. VERB PHRASE:
Mitchell was playing football. **But really wanted to run cross-country.** (lacks subject)

Rewrite:
Mitchell was playing football, but really wanted to run cross-country.

or

Even though Mitchell was playing football, he really wanted to run cross-country.

6. DEPENDENT CLAUSE:
   Randy baked in the hot sun, broiling both sides of his body. **Until he**
   realized that he was overdoing it. (has a subject and predicate but is made
   subordinate by **until**)

Rewrite:
   Randy baked in the hot sun, broiling both sides of his body, until he
   realized that he was overdoing it.

or

   Until he realized that he was overdoing it, Randy baked in the hot sun,
   broiling both sides of his body.

7. FRAGMENT WITH A RELATIVE PRONOUN:
   The seventh grade class toured the science museum. **Which was showing an**
   exhibit of nineteenth-century inventions. (has a subject and predicate but is
   made subordinate by **which**)

Rewrite:
   The seventh grade class toured the science museum which was showing an
   exhibit of nineteenth-century inventions.

or

   The seventh grade class toured the science museum; an exhibit on
   nineteenth-century inventions was showing.

8. NOUN AND MODIFIER:
   The clerk behind the counter. He was trying to sell the most expensive
   jewelry. (lacks verb)

Rewrite:
   The clerk behind the counter was trying to sell the most expensive jewelry.

or

   The clerk was behind the counter, trying to sell the most expensive jewelry.

NAME _____ DATE _____

Identify each of the following as either a sentence or a fragment. If it is not a sentence, perform the necessary corrections to make it one. Remember, there is no one right way to correct a fragment.

Example: When I go home for vacation. FRAGMENT
When I go home for vacation, **I will study.**

1. Whenever Fred leaves.

2. Running the final race.

3. Where you see the dogs playing.

4. That old man is crazy.

5. That I must not worry.

6. Sometimes they visit here.

7. If you want to succeed in business without spending too much time.

8. To have dinner early.

9. As if he never wanted to hear it again.

10. Whether Canadians wanted it or not.

11. In order to win the scholarship.

12. When the earthquake occurred and the people left.

13. The children had nightmares about snakes.

14. Before the tulips bloomed and the trees budded.

15. While the tourists waited behind and the guide went into the hotel.

2   Signals of Fragments

The following words and phrases often signal fragments which are dependent clauses. Be sure to double-check sentences beginning with these words to make certain they are complete sentences.

WORDS THAT OFTEN BEGIN ADVERB CLAUSES:

after	than
although	though
as, as if, as long, as though	unless
because	until
before	whatever
if	when, whenever
in order that	where, wherever
since	whether
so that	while

WORDS THAT OFTEN BEGIN ADJECTIVE CLAUSES:

that	who
when	whom
where	whose
which	

WORDS THAT OFTEN BEGIN NOUN CLAUSES:

how	whomever
if	whatever
that	when
what	where
whichever	whether
whoever	why

WORDS THAT OFTEN INTRODUCE SENTENCES BUT CAN SIGNAL FRAGMENTS:

also	like
especially	mainly
for instance/for example	provided/provided that
just/just as	such/such as

NAME _____   DATE _____

Identify each of the following as either a sentence or a fragment. If it is not a sentence, perform the necessary corrections to make it one.

Example: When I go home for vacation. FRAGMENT
          When I go home for vacation, **I will study.**

1. Begging all the time.

2. Whatever Jane says.

3. Although Kip doesn't eat much.

4. Let them be.

5. What I saw.

6. With a pug nose and big feet.

7. Underneath the plum tree, sitting in the breeze.

8. What are you doing?

9. I don't know.

10. Until it snows.

11. Jumping up and down.

12. Sometime I'll go.

13. They don't really dance.

14. Before you leave here.

15. That's disgusting.

Some of the following are not sentences. Locate any fragments and correct them in the space provided.

Example: Although Jane and Mary were together at the movies and then a party.
Although Jane and Mary were together at the movies and then a party, **they were still angry with each other.**

1. Many people think that jogging is good for you. Although some doctors have proven that jogging can be harmful to older adults just beginning.

2. Too many students try to drop their English classes.

3. To prepare for the final exams. George studied history, English, and sociology at least ten hours a day.

4. Jill doesn't know what to do. If Jack doesn't come home exactly at five o'clock.

5. The young girl, who has short blond hair and who is always talking to the mail clerk.

6. Don't get me upset. I have to present this paper at 1:00. And be at a cocktail party at 4:00.

7. I really don't see how she's going to be able to race. Limping around the way she is.

8. Most people want to marry someone who is supportive and kind. A spouse who will share the good and bad times.

9. Get out of here! You were the one who insulted my mother. After she accidentally broke one of your glasses.

10. Trying to act concerned. She didn't really deceive any members of the committee.

11. The new electronics store provides a complete line of video equipment. For instance, the new video cassettes.

12. The library was going to offer evening reading sessions. Provided enough senior citizens signed up.

13. Twenty-nine students attended the symposium on computer skills. Trying to update their computer background.

14. The owner of the tree nursery was growing tropical trees with great success. Such as, the date palm.

15. Whatever the case. The judge reviews the pertinent laws and codes.

Correct the following paragraph by finding and incorporating the fragments properly. (7 fragments)

The class discussion on Jean-Paul Sartre's *Being and Nothingness* proved exciting and productive. As the instructor allowed students to present their own views about existential existence. Linda indicated that she just couldn't believe all that "bunk." Because of her strict Catholic upbringing. Although Frank was hesitant to admit it. He finally said that maybe there's something to what Sartre proposes. Which is applicable to modern society. All the class members readily accepted the difficulty of Sartre's philosophy. When read for an introductory philosophy course. But as the instructor said. "Getting an education is not an easy task. Since you will use it the rest of your lives." Everyone agreed.

Grammar

COMMA SPLICE AND FUSED SENTENCE

1 Fused Sentence

Fused sentences are not as common in writing as are comma splices. But when they do occur, they are even more of a stumbling block than comma splices because the main ideas are not separated to allow the reader to distinguish between two ideas. Instead, readers have to stumble through the "sentence" several times and try to create their own meaning of the ideas. Note the example of a fused sentence below:

The fire on Belmont Street was started by arsonists they escaped injury.

2 Comma Splice

A comma splice occurs when independent clauses are joined with a comma only. This structure always occurs in compound sentences. A comma splice is not only an error in grammar but also an error in punctuation. See the example below:

The fire on Belmont Street was started by arsonists, they escaped injury.

Both fused sentences and comma splices can be remedied in the following ways.

A. Independent clauses can be joined by a coordinate conjunction (**and**, **but**, **or**, **for**, **nor**, **yet**, **so**) with a comma before the conjunction.

The fire on Belmont Street was started by arsonists, **and** they escaped injury.

B. Or independent clauses can be joined by a semicolon. When a semicolon is used, it must have independent clauses on both sides of it. (See Items **66** and **67** on the use of the semicolon.)

The fire on Belmont Street was started by arsonists; they escaped injury.

C. Or independent clauses can be joined by subordinating one of the independent clauses, using a subordinating conjunction or a relative pronoun.

Some subordinate conjunctions

after	how	until
although	if	what
as	in order that	whatever
as if	provided that	when
as far as	since	whenever
as long as	so that	where
as soon as	that	wherever
because	though	whether
before	unless	while
		why

Relative pronouns

that	whoever
which	whom
who	whomever

The fire on Belmont Street was started by arsonists **who** escaped injury.

D. Finally, a comma splice or fused sentence can be corrected by simply making two sentences of the independent clauses.

The fire on Belmont Street was started by arsonists. They escaped injury.

NAME _____ DATE _____

All of the following sentences are either fused sentences or comma splices. Indicate whether each item is either a fused sentence or a comma splice, and correct it, using one of the previously mentioned solutions.

Example: In the following exercise you may find comma splices, you need to correct them.

In the following exercise you may find comma splices. You need to correct them.

or

When you find comma splices in the following exercise, you need to correct them.

1. Margaret, Debby, and George found Derek in the library, he was reading *Walden*.

2. The hounds ran over the shrubs, around the pond, and into the woods, the rabbit had no chance at all.

3. Up to the government building marched the union protestors, singing and shouting they ended the march.

4. After the game, the team rested on the sidelines some drank lemonade.

5. The psychiatrist listened carefully for many hours the patient talked.

6. Later in the day they rode horses the sun set slowly.

7. Everyone ate quickly, after the play they fell asleep.

8. Long after dawn the fog held tight to the mountain tops, it hugged the crags.

9. Come home with me, give me your hand you are my friend.

10. The deer ran in front of the car the brakes screeched, Rachel screamed.

Some of the following sentences are correct. If they are, then place a *C* next to that sentence. If, however, they are incorrect, make the necessary changes, using one of the four methods.

1. Bob went home. Linda stayed with Mary, and Frank left the country.

2. The faculty voted Millie the scholarship money, after the meeting was over she resigned from the organization.

3. The boy deflated the tires of his brother's bicycle all by himself, his father reinflated them.

4. The angry Indians chased the cavalry far across the mountains, before dawn the cavalry regrouped and attacked.

5. Write carefully and clearly indent paragraphs punctuate as necessary.

6. Uncle Sam needs you; you need Uncle Sam.

7. He started the motorboat and rode quickly after his brother, the boat took him rapidly out of sight into the sun it sank suddenly hiding the disappearing silhouette.

8. The city was confusing with its sights and sounds Roberta was unprepared for this excitement.

9. The storm destroyed all before it and left the people sobbing in the mud.

10. The fire truck reached the fire too late, the house burned down. The embers glowed all night.

NAME _____ DATE _____

In the paragraph below you will find a given number of fused sentences and comma splices. Correct them with the necessary punctuation and conjunctions.

The women of today are a larger portion of the work force than women of fifty years ago, and thus have more say-so in the future of American society. Today's women are not content to stay home taking care of domestic chores they want to get involved in community services, to pursue full-time careers, and to be a part of growing America. The women of today contribute a great deal to the development of a better society, through their efforts to protect their own consumer interests, they help all of America's purchasing population. They demand better health facilities, the young, middle aged, and the elderly all benefit. Women's efforts in presenting competency in public office have helped revivify the importance of the democratic ideal, this helps pave the way for future citizens. All in all modern women have created a better society in which to live men have helped too.

(Have you found two fused sentences and three comma splices?)

Grammar

ITEM 32 (SEE ALSO ITEM 45)

CONFUSING SENTENCES

A confusing sentence is one whose meaning is unclear or scrambled because of some flaw in word choice or arrangement of words. Such a sentence might be called "non-English" because it violates the rules and conventions of the English language; word choice is incompatible or inappropriate for a certain context; sentences do not follow conventional English sentence patterns. Incompatible words or improper arrangement of words often leads to confusion in meaning which cannot be clarified without knowing the writer's intention.

For example, note the following sentence whose meaning is confusing because of incompatible word choice. Pay attention to the boldface words and phrases.

One aspect of morality is your **beliefs** in premarital sex.

The question is whether the writer is talking about only one aspect of a person's morality or about several aspects of one's feelings about premarital sex. The confusion results when the writer links, by use of verb BE, a singular idea (**One aspect**) with a plural idea (**beliefs**). These words are incompatible because one is singular and the other is plural. In this context they both must be singular (**One aspect of morality is your belief** . . .) or plural (**Some aspects of morality are your beliefs** . . .).

The following example is confusing because the arrangement of words gives the impression that some important link is missing. Thus, the reader is unsure of the meaning.

Early in the day, the bus full of people the tour left for San Francisco.

Confusion results by missing the link between **the bus full of people** and **the tour.** The conventional word arrangement could link **the tour** to some other element in the sentence by use of a preposition. The following revisions clarify the sentence's meaning:

Early in the day, the bus full of people left on a San Francisco tour.

or

Early in the day, the bus full of people on the tour left for San Francisco.

Rewrite the following confusing sentences in two ways that will clarify possible meanings. After each revision, explain the meanings that you were trying to convey.

1. After several minutes of reeling, the fish came to the surface.

2. The visible comparison of one minority group to another exempt from life's conflicts insomuch as the individual's ideas, moral, and beliefs are concerned.

3. Another disorder is the state of characters of whom are strewn about in disarray.

4. For example, loneliness to a person can mean being on a crowded street with ten to twenty people standing there with him on that one, single street corner.

5. I feel that maybe the reason this is that God felt this was needed to set His people up establishing and keeping His covenant with His people Israel.

6. Social attitudes were directed toward righteous people which projected an immaculate-type society.

7. Until the final remark by Oliver, does the mood of the story pick up again.

8. An individual wanting to move himself from one stature in life to another is regarded as gratification rather than it being regarded as it was in medieval times.

9. The events of *Portrait of a Lady,* Isabel relates to us, appears from a different light than from her ideas when she was younger.

10. Upon entering the room the thing that grabs your attention are all the desks cluttered around the room.

11. College is an atmosphere for adults.

12. Whether the poem is successful or not is extremely difficult to do.

13. Not necessarily does he need to be directly in focus with it, but as a member of society, he is concerned with himself as a member of society, he concerned and mainly nothing else.

14. Reds are aliens under the suspicion of sympathy with the Communist régime.

15. It was 7:45 that morning—a morning I will always remember as being drenched with fear and emotion.

The following passage has numerous problems with sentence structure. Make the necessary revisions to correct sentence fragments, comma splices, and fused or confusing sentences. You may have to reword the sentences in order to achieve readable prose.

Finally in August, the Edwards family left Nebraska and arrived at the point of their departure into the Montana wilderness. They rested a day before beginning the week-long trip, they would search for traces of the bighorn sheep. On the trip everything went according to plan and on schedule. The weather began pleasant enough but after two days it turned rainy. On the third day, nearly the halfway point on their trip. The weather suddenly turned cold this was accompanied by a series of violent thunderstorms. After the rainstorms, a light brushing of snow coated the wet trail. And made traveling awkward and slightly dangerous. This really put a damper on the Edwards' trip.

Realizing their potential danger. They made decisions about their immediate return. Their progress to this point had been leisurely, by speeding up they could make a return trip in two days. In order to do that, they would have to lighten their loads and leave behind unnecessary equipment. Like the extra tent and extra shovel and stove. The camera tripod and unnecessary toiletries could be left behind the rangers could recover their belongings later. Bill figured they had better take all the food in case of emergency, Janet determined a new route that would be shorter though more rugged and steep.

After an uneasy ordeal, they finally arrived at the ranger station two and a half days later. On the trip down, Joseph had slipped and sprained his ankle. Requiring first aid treatment. It was good that Dorothy had prepared for such emergencies. For without her attention, Joseph would not have been able to make it down the steep path. The trip was a memorable one for the Edwards family because each took seriously the responsibility of caring for the other family members they had prepared carefully for unforeseen emergencies.

Style

SENTENCE VARIETY

---

1   Types of Sentences

There are four types of sentences determined by the kind and number of clauses they contain: **simple**, **compound**, **complex**, **compound-complex**.

A **simple** sentence has one independent clause and no dependent (subordinate) clauses. Even though simple sentences contain only one main clause, the subject and/or predicate may be compound. The following examples show the various types of simple sentences:

      SUBJECT   PREDICATE
Georgette framed the pictures.

      COMPOUND SUBJECT   PREDICATE
Georgette and Philip framed the pictures.

      SUBJECT   COMPOUND PREDICATE
Georgette framed the pictures and sold them to merchandise firms.

A **compound** sentence contains two or more independent clauses and no dependent clauses. These clauses are coordinated (joined) in four ways:

1) **coordinate conjunctions**—and, but, nor, or, for, yet
2) **correlative conjunctions**—either . . . or, neither . . . nor, not only . . . but also, both . . . and

3) **conjunctive adverbs**—however, therefore, then, also, consequently
4) **internal punctuation**—semicolon (Often the semicolon is used preceding a conjunctive adverb in order to create a more complete bond between the independent clauses.)

At first James lost his way **but** he eventually found the exit.
(coordinate conjunction)

Either Frank lost his way **or** he couldn't find the exit.
(correlative conjunction)

James lost his way; **however**, he eventually found the exit.
(conjunctive adverb and semicolon)

A **complex** sentence contains one independent clause and one or more subordinate clauses. Remember that even though it has a subject and predicate, a subordinate clause must be connected to the main clause of the sentence (see Item **29**). The connectors relating the subordinate clause to the main clause are either relative pronouns (**who, which, that**) or subordinate conjunctions (**after, although, as, because, before, if, since, so, though, until, when, where, while**). Since subordinate clauses may be used as nouns, as adjectives, or as adverbs, it is important for you to consider carefully the meanings of these connectors. You should choose the one which shows the proper relationship between the two clauses. The following examples demonstrate various subordinate clauses:

That she merits a pay raise is clear from her many commendations.
(Relative pronoun **that** introduces subordinate clause used as a noun, subject of the sentence.)

The farmers will retill the soil **after they fertilize it**.
(Subordinate conjunction introduces subordinate clause used as an adverb denoting time.)

The bankers **who fired thirty employees** were sued for discrimination against minorities.
(Relative pronoun **who** introduces subordinate clause used as an adjective modifying **bankers**.)

A **compound-complex** sentence is a combination of the two types mentioned above. It may have two or more main clauses and one or more subordinate clauses. The following example shows a possible combination:

Since the earthquake struck so suddenly (subordinate clause), **many of the visitors were frightened** (independent clause), *but when an explanation was given* (subordinate clause), **they felt more comfortable** (independent clause).

2 Methods to Ensure Sentence Variety

In order to create sentence variety in your writing, you must determine which type of sentence best presents your intended meaning. Often this means combining sentences in order to eliminate monotony and repetition and to emphasize main ideas. There are four basic transformations which allow you to revise sentences for variety: **shifting** (rearranging), **deleting** (omitting), **combining** (compounding), **embedding** (subordinating).

Generally, **shifting** and **deleting** are the techniques used when combining two or more sentences whose elements are repetitious. By deleting extraneous verbiage and condensing ideas into modifying units (adjectives, adverbs, phrases, clauses), more direct sentences are created. Note the ways in which the following simple sentences are combined into a new sentence with clearer emphasis and less wordiness.

Simple Sentences:
1. The museum purchased a painting.
2. The painting was rare.
3. The director of the museum was pleased.

The museum purchased a painting which was rare.

or

The museum purchased a rare painting.

In both combinations, excess verbiage is eliminated (deleted) and the modifying idea—rare—is rearranged. In the first combination, the relative clause **which was rare** modifies **painting**; in the second combination, the adjective **rare** modifies **painting**.

By **combining** simple sentences you can create compound sentences. Note how simple sentence **3** is combined with the simple sentence from above:

The museum purchased a rare painting **and** the director of the museum was pleased. (coordinate conjunction **and**)

or

The museum purchased a rare painting; **therefore**, the director of the museum was pleased. (conjunctive adverb **therefore** and semicolon)

Embedding is used to subordinate one or more clauses, thus creating a complex sentence. For example, in the very first combination of sentences **1**

and **2**, a relative clause **which was rare** is subordinate to the main clause and acts as an adjective modifying **painting**. The three original simple sentences can again be **combined**, **embedded**, and **rearranged** to create a complex sentence.

The director of the museum was pleased **because** the museum purchased a rare painting. (conjunctive adverb **because** signals a subordinate clause)

or

Since the museum purchased a rare painting, the director was pleased. (conjunctive adverb **since** signals a subordinate clause)

By varying sentence length and word order, you can create prose which is interesting and easy to read. For example, by interspersing shorter, simple sentences among longer, complex sentences, you will break the monotony of a longer passage. The shorter sentences will highlight and emphasize important ideas because they will change the movement established by longer sentences.

Changing the word order in sentences will also avoid a S-V-O pattern that creates boring prose when used repetitiously; a more varied rhythm will regenerate your reader's interest. Both of these techniques for creating sentence variety can be achieved by using the sentence combining discussed above. Note the following passage and its revision:

> The South Beach fans were excited about their baseball team's standing. They were second in their division. This placing tied them with the Riverside team. They would play in a play-off game. If South Beach won the play-off game, they could go on to the division tournament. The tournament would be in Columbus, Ohio. The top two teams from the Y and Z divisions would go. They would play one another in a round-robin tournament.

REVISION

> The South Beach fans were excited about their baseball team's standing. Tieing with Riverside, they placed second in their division. There would be a play-off game and if South Beach won, they would go to the division tournament in Columbus, Ohio. There, the top two teams from the Y and Z divisions would play one another in a round-robin tournament.

Using the techniques described, combine the following groups of sentences. Make as many combinations as possible and consider the variations in emphases with each combination.

1. The plane crashed.
   The crash was in Wyoming.

2. Rona was at the track meet.
   Rona was a timekeeper.

3. The fire raged.
   The fire was out of control.
   The firefighters were frightened.

4. The book is red.
   The title is *Paradise Lost*.
   The book is in the library.

5. The teacher made the assignment.
   The assignment was for a composition class.
   The assignment was due on Friday.

6. Peter cast his fly.
Peter cast into the stream.
Peter snagged his line.
The line was on a bush.

7. Janet walked along the path.
Jim walked along the path.
The path was moonlit.
The path was in the woods.

8. Jed was on the football team.
Jed was the quarterback.
The football team lost games.
The football team won one game.

9. Fourteen high school students went to New York City.
Two chaperones went to New York City.
New York City is an exciting place.
Millions of people live in New York City.

10. The tanker ship sped through the waves.
The waves were twenty feet high.
The wind howled.
The thunder was frightening.
The lightning was frightening.

NAME _____ DATE _____

Combine the following groups of sentences. Make as many combinations as possible considering the variations in emphases each combination will produce.

1. The bookstore owner lived above the store.
   The store was old.
   The store was well-established.
   The bookstore owner had three cats.

2. The children returned from school.
   The children were playing with their dog.
   The dog's name was Skippy.
   Their dog was frisky.

3. There were twelve of the fifteen elected council members.
   The twelve members opposed the bond issue.
   The bond issue was created recently.
   The bond issue was to raise more money for schools.

4. The ladies met Tuesday afternoons.
   The ladies met in the church hall.
   The ladies brought their sewing materials.
   The quilting stand was in the church hall.
   The group formed a quilting bee last fall.

5. The storm went unnoticed by the weather service.
   The weather service did not send out any warnings.
   The storm turned into a hurricane.
   The hurricane surprised the islanders.
   The hurricane damaged the islanders' homes.
   The damage was extensive.

6. The trip north was painful.
   Marvin felt the pain.
   Marvin was returning to his hometown.
   All of Marvin's family was gone now.
   Only Marvin's house remained.
   The house held all of Marvin's childhood memories.

7. Brad met his friends.
   They met at the golf course.
   The weather was beautiful.
   It was a day full of sunshine.

8. There were many deer in the valley.
   The deer grazed peacefully.
   The deer were startled.
   The rangers' helicopter flew low.
   The rangers were searching for an injured buck.

9. The report was lengthy.
   Mary gave the report.
   The report was presented at the board meeting.
   The board members wanted to raise employees' salaries.
   The report outlines the board's responsibility to its employees.

10. Spring was around the corner.
    Tulips were blooming.
    Lilacs were budding.
    The children played in the soft rain.
    The rain was warm.

Using the techniques described, combine the following groups of sentences. Then group the combined sentences into one paragraph rearranging the sentences, if necessary, to make the paragraph coherent.

1. The aliens entered the *Enterprise*.
   The aliens came through cracks.
   The cracks were in the engine room.

2. Captain Kirk commands the *Enterprise*.
   The Captain was surprised.
   Captain Kirk saw an alien vessel.

3. Spock listened to the aliens.
   Spock interpreted for the aliens.
   The aliens wanted to escape.
   The escape was to Earth.

4. A Red Alert was necessary.
   Battle stations were taken.
   The *Enterprise* crew acted without fear.

5. The aliens were humanoid.
   The aliens were greenish.
   The aliens were transparent.
   The aliens appeared three feet tall.
   The aliens had a language.
   The language had peculiar sounds.

6. Spock was his calm self.
   Spock was his usual self.
   Spock was able to communicate.
   The communication was with the aliens.
   The aliens seemed pleased.

NAME _____ DATE _____

Rearrange the sentences into a coherent paragraph.

NAME _____ DATE _____

Combine the following groups of sentences. Then group the combined sentences into one paragraph rearranging the sentences, if necessary, to make the paragraph coherent.

1. The reporter was angry.
   The reporter was finally announced.
   The reporter was ushered into the Governor's office.
   The office was plush.

2. The reporter left the office.
   The reporter could present an outlook.
   The outlook was brighter.
   The outlook was for the taxpayers.

3. The newspaper reporter made an appointment.
   The appointment was with the Governor.
   The appointment was an interview.
   The interview was about a new proposal.
   The proposal was a tax increase.

4. The reporter arrived for the meeting.
   The reporter was on time.
   The Governor was busy.
   The reporter was kept waiting.
   The wait was for two hours.

5. The reporter discovered something.
   The discovery was during the interview.
   The discovery was faulty information.
   The information said the Governor was for a tax increase.
   The Governor was for a tax decrease.

Rearrange the sentences into a coherent paragraph.

Coordinate the following pairs of sentences using the appropriate connector and, if necessary, punctuation.

1. Ice covered the streets.
Snow still fell.

2. The zoo had a new arboretum.
The park planted a new flower garden.

3. In June, forty-five of the sixty graduates already had jobs.
Last year, only half of the graduates were employed by June.

4. The Smith estate was for sale.
The Smith land was to be subdivided.

5. The lantern went out.
The room was dark.

Combine the following pairs of sentences, subordinating one clause and using the appropriate connector and punctuation.

1. Alex would return to Europe.
Alex had enough money.

2. The luggage was left behind.
The luggage was too heavy.

3. The installation of lights at this baseball field was successful.
Many other fields followed suit.

4. The train stops at Omaha.
Many passengers will get off.

5. The store owner was a man.
The store owner was fair with his employees.

NAME _____ DATE _____

Combine the following groups of sentences. Carefully assess the meaning of each independent clause and decide whether to coordinate the clauses, to subordinate one of them, or to use one of them as a modifier. Remember to place punctuation in its proper place.

1. The car crashed into the telephone pole.
   The heavy snow created poor visibility.

2. Friday afternoons were always pleasant for Marie.
   Marie had tea with her grandmother.

3. Harry rented a canoe.
   Dottie rented a motorboat.

4. Heavy rains fell on the plains states.
   Many rivers were above flood stage.

5. The school bus went to the east side of town.
   The school bus couldn't go to the north side of town.

6. Three of the little leaguers were sick.
   Two of the little leaguers were on vacation.
   There was an important game on Sunday.

7. Norman found out his test scores.
   Norman was disappointed.
   Norman felt rejected.

8. Overnight, branches had fallen from the trees.
Many branches were on the ground.
Some branches knocked out power lines.

9. The baby sitter had a great responsibility.
Taking care of five infants was a difficult task.

10. The Jones Plumbing Company was busy installing plumbing in the new office building.
The new office building would house thirty-five doctors and dentists.
The building would open on September 1.

Style

ITEM 40

WRONG WORD AND
FAULTY PREDICATION

1   Wrong Word

Some words have similar sounds and can be confused easily. Always be sure you have selected the word that has the precise meaning you want. If you are not sure about a word's meaning, look it up in the dictionary before using it.

> Sherlock Holmes was always able to **deduct** the solution of a case from a mass of specific evidence.

Rewrite:
> Sherlock Holmes was always able to **deduce** the solution of a case from a mass of specific evidence.
> (**Deduct** means to *subtract*; what the writer really means to convey is *to figure out by reasoning*.)

2   Unfamiliar Words

Words that are unfamiliar can also be misused. Do not use words just because they are big or sound learned. Words often have particular associations and can be used only in specific contexts. Be sure you know the proper context for any new words you include in your writing.

Beethoven has become **notorious** for his symphonies and quartets.

Rewrite:
Beethoven has become **famous** for this symphonies and quartets.
(The word **notorious** is usually associated with *unfavorable* public attention or renown.)

---

3   Faulty Predication

Part of writing clear and understandable sentences depends on giving your reader reliable signals. Faulty predication occurs when the signals given at the beginning of a sentence do not correspond to what actually follows; the connection between subject and predicate becomes illogical. Subject and predicate should match grammatically and make good sense together.

Pollution and energy conservation are two of our most urgent problems.

Rewrite:
Pollution and **the lack of** efficient energy conservation are two of our most urgent problems.

A comma fault is when two independent clauses are linked only by a comma.

Rewrite:
A comma fault **occurs** when two independent clauses are linked only by a comma.

One particularly common type of faulty predication occurs in comparison. In a comparative sentence, you should include both things being compared and make sure that you have not compared two items illogically.

I think every human being is different.

Rewrite:
I think every human being is different **from all the others.** (Both items being compared, each person and everybody else, need to be included in the sentence to make the comparison complete.)

More dentists use Fluorobrite than any other toothpaste.

Rewrite:
Dentists use Fluorobrite more than any other toothpaste. (The illogical comparison in the first sentence compares dentists to toothpaste; the second sentence compares the use of one toothpaste to the use of the others.)

NAME _____ DATE _____

In the following sentences, underline the word in parentheses that best completes the meaning of the sentence. Write a brief definition of the word you did *not* underline.

Example: Yesterday was (quite, quiet) hot—96°F in the shade!
quiet: still, making no noise

1. Her quick, nervous gestures (implied, implicated) that she was uneasy.

2. I don't know anyone (beside, besides) Jane who owns a bright purple car.

3. Did he (accept, except) a job in Chicago?

4. The (effects, affects) of the storm were evident everywhere.

5. The senator said he opposed the new tax bill on (principal, principle).

6. He's always (adverse, averse) to any sort of change in his habits.

7. Jack can't eat snails; to look at them makes him feel (nauseated, nauseous).

8. While you were away, we painted the dining room a (vivid, livid) yellow.

9. I cannot (comprehend, apprehend) the problems in my mathematics textbook.

10. The fact that the room is small does not (detract, distract) from its comfort.

11. The pictures of hurricane damage in Florida (affected, effected) Marie strongly.

12. In her speech, she (alluded, eluded) to the recent electoral scandal.

13. The (climactic, climatic) event of the school year is the all-school picnic on the beach.

14. The mixture of color and pattern in that mural offends my (ascetic, aesthetic) sense.

15. Joe has a (luxuriant, luxurious), brown, silky beard.

NAME _____ DATE _____

One sentence in each of these pairs uses the underlined word incorrectly. Circle the letter of the correct sentence, then supply a better word in place of the incorrectly used word.

Example: (a.) He left the country, <u>ostensibly</u> to improve his health.
      b. The bird on the lawn was <u>ostensibly</u> a robin. **apparently**

1. a. After only a <u>cursory</u> examination, the expert pronounced the painting a forgery.
  b. The second-graders practiced their <u>cursory</u> penmanship.

2. a. The police <u>suspect</u> that the butler committed the murder, but they have not accused him of it yet.
  b. I <u>suspect</u> my sister's arrival any time now.

3. a. Generally, his comments are <u>irrelevant</u> to the main topic of discussion.
  b. Her opinion of my decision is perfectly <u>irrelevant</u> to me.

4. a. I certainly don't intend to <u>refute</u> your right to your own beliefs.
  b. It isn't enough to state your own case; you must also <u>refute</u> your opponent's arguments.

5. a. Whenever anyone praises John, he shows his <u>implacable</u> shyness.
  b. Mr. Jones eyed his crabgrass with <u>implacable</u> hatred.

6. a. Poppa Marco's gives the most <u>expedient</u> pizza delivery in town.
  b. Cheating may be <u>expedient</u>, if you haven't studied for the exam, but it's certainly not ethical.

7. a. I suggested to Jerry that we go camping this weekend, but he was totally <u>disinterested</u>.
  b. We need to find a well-trained but <u>disinterested</u> judge for the debate.

8. a. Summer heat always completely <u>enervates</u> me; I just want to lie around.
  b. Cold showers in the morning <u>enervate</u> me so that I feel as if I could accomplish anything.

9. a. Jo received so much <u>fulsome</u> praise for her dancing that she was almost tempted to stop performing in public.
  b. On our last visit home, our mother cooked wonderful, <u>fulsome</u> meals.

10. a. Connie feels <u>ambivalent</u> right now about taking a summer job or attending summer school.
  b. I'm glad to see that Martin is <u>ambivalent</u> again, now that his cast is off.

Rewrite the following sentences to correct the faulty predication.

1. The only experience I have of small children is living for three months with my brother's family.

2. Because it was raining yesterday is why my front lawn is flooded.

3. The concept of negative numbers is where I get confused.

4. People in rural areas often hold more conservative ideas than urban areas.

5. Children dying from diphtheria have been almost completely prevented these days.

6. Personification is when inanimate objects are given human qualities.

7. We hope that people in the future will base their societies more on peace and justice than people today.

8. Having enough time and sloppy organization are problems students need to overcome when they take exams.

9. A feeling of belonging is an experience many people join organizations for.

10. The best part of the movie was where the hero chased the villain through the New York sewers.

Style

ITEMS 41 and 42

PRECISE AND APPROPRIATE WORDS

---

1 Using precise words

The use of vague or overly general words will make your writing unclear and dull. In order to convey your ideas clearly and exactly, you must choose precise, specific words.

The class came up with some **good** ideas for class projects.

Rewrite:
The class came up with some **original but inexpensive** ideas for class projects.

In the following sentences, notice the difference in meaning made by a change in one precise word.

The pianist **grinned** at his audience.

The pianist **smirked** at his audience.

2   Using appropriate words

A word is used inappropriately if it does not suit its surroundings. Do not mix formal and informal language or introduce words that change the tone of a sentence. Always use words that are consistent with the occasion, the audience, and the mood of your writing.

> I would like to say that the people of this town have treated me hospitably, courteously, and **downright neighborly.**

Rewrite:

> I would like to say that the people of this town have treated me hospitably, courteously, and **pleasantly.**

> Today, children, we're going to the museum without taking our **writing implements.**

Rewrite:

> Today, children, we're going to the museum without taking our **pencils.**

NAME _____ DATE _____

Find two more specific words for each of the following general words.

Example: **sport**   tennis   basketball

1. **artist**   _____   _____

2. **walk** (v.)   _____   _____

3. **happy**   _____   _____

4. **plant** (n.)   _____   _____

5. **look** (v.)   _____   _____

6. **say**   _____   _____

7. **tool**   _____   _____

8. **sad**   _____   _____

9. **vehicle**   _____   _____

10. **sound** (n.)   _____   _____

In the following sentences replace the underlined vague or overly general words with more specific words.

Example: Take that thing out of the kitchen.
             Take that **frog** out of the kitchen.

1. There are some nice things in that department store window.

2. With a little practice, John can play most things.

3. Our room looks much brighter now with all that stuff on the walls.

4. Sally is a good child.

5. Actually, Frank is a very nice guy.

6. The litter on our city streets is a disgrace; we all ought to get out and do something.

7. I think my biology teacher is great.

8. David went to see the movie twice because he thought it was so meaningful.

9. When we're together, my sister and I always have a lot of fun.

10. Walking in the hills is a good experience.

NAME _____ DATE _____

In the following sentences, circle the more appropriate word or words, according to the sentence context.

Example: Some days, the whole world seems to grow suddenly silent, huge, grey clouds form in the west, and a low, distant (burp, (rumble)) of thunder faintly reaches us.

1. His philosophy is based on meditation, integration of the self into the rhythms of the natural world, and (hanging loose, serene acceptance of all occurrences).

2. When we were kids, my brother and I used to fool around down by the creek, skipping rocks, wading or paddling in the mud, and picking up (big snails, large spiral gastropod mollusks).

3. It is not terribly difficult to learn the rudiments of watercolor painting, but to master the nuances of the art (requires constant discipline, takes a lot of effort).

4. Mary and I like it here—not too much noise, neighborly folks, a down-home feeling, lots of space, and (a salubrious atmosphere, a nice climate).

5. Possibly you may increase your prestige among the socially elite of your community by employing their linguistic standards, but don't (expect this always to be true, bet your shirt on it).

6. (Before you start washing, Before you initiate the cleansing of) a St. Bernard, you need to have ready a gallon of dog shampoo, a strong hose, and seven neighborhood kids in bathing suits.

7. Now, children, let's draw pictures of those beautiful (feathered creatures flocking convivially over the lawn, birds hopping around together on the lawn).

8. It's always easy to put off my English homework, but finally I have to (buckle down and get it done, exert myself to complete the task).

9. The student seeking to enter medical school over the next three years may find tuition costs prohibitive and competition for scholarships (quite stringent, a knock-down, drag-out fight).

10. One theory to explain the recent heavy rainfall over the U.S. suggests that volcanic eruptions have (increased the normal amount of, put a whole lot more) particulates in the atmosphere.

Write sentences of your own, one for each of the paired words. Be sure to use the word in an appropriate context.

1. avaricious–stingy

2. mentally ill–crazy

3. particle–little piece

4. slender–skinny

5. sleep–snooze

6. intelligent–smart

7. err–make a mistake

8. abbreviate–cut short

9. braid–pigtail

10. interrupt–butt in

Style

ITEM 43

USING THE PROPER IDIOM

Many expressions in American English, particularly those involving prepositions, cannot be understood by just knowing the meanings of their individual words. These expressions result from custom in the language and must simply be learned as the unique way native speakers express a particular idea. For example,

Joe often takes afternoon naps <u>to make up for</u> working until 2:00 a.m.

In compounded phrases, if a preposition does not fit idiomatically with both elements of the compound, the appropriate preposition for each element must be used.

He likes to read and talk about philosophical issues.

(The preposition **about** fits idiomatically with both **to read** and [to] **talk.**)

No other dessert is better than or equal to my mother's chocolate pie.

(In this sentence, **than** fits with **better** but does not fit with **equal**. Therefore, an appropriate preposition—in this case **to**—must be used with **equal.**)

NAME _____ DATE _____

Rewrite the following sentences, correcting unidiomatic expressions.

1. Advertisements produce much of their effect by making an appeal at people's emotions.

2. I think hamsters are inferior than dogs as pets.

3. In Dr. Adam's class, the study of paragraphing is subsequent and dependent on the study of sentence structure.

4. Shall we meet to Jim's house tonight?

5. Every evening he listens the radio.

6. How long have you been waiting against an answer to your letter?

7. Will you introduce me with your mother?

8. The orchestra began to playing a rousing march.

9. My father succeeded to learn Italian at the age of eighty-two.

10. He's certainly capable to murder anyone he hated.

Indicate a preposition that can be used idiomatically with the following words. Then use each phrase in a sentence.

1. refer—

2. different—

3. in proportion—

4. similar—

5. associate (v.)—

6. disassociate—

7. adjust—

8. disagree—

9. insist—

10. correlate—

NAME _____ DATE _____

Some common verbs can express a number of different meanings, depending on the prepositions following them. For each word here give two prepositions that influence its meaning and use each in a sentence.

   1. run—

   2. pass—

   3. take—

   4. turn—

   5. call—

   6. break—

   7. bring—

   8. go—

   9. get—

10. throw—

Style

TRITE EXPRESSIONS

Phrases that have been overused and worn out should be avoided as much as possible. Their meaning is usually stereotyped and generalized, and they have very little force of expression or power to evoke thought. In place of trite expressions, use clear, direct language or original figures of speech. Slang phrases, in particular, can become trite very quickly.

NAME _____ DATE _____

Underline the trite expressions in the following sentences. Rewrite each as clearly and simply as possible, choosing your words carefully.

Example: When I came back from my hike, I was <u>hungry as a bear.</u>
When I came back from my hike, I was **ravenous.**

1. John told us his better half couldn't come to the party because of a slight indisposition owing to her interesting condition.

2. My uncle is eighty-five years old, but he's still as fit as a fiddle.

3. Forty-two people came to Mary's surprise party and a good time was had by all.

4. We are going to attend the last sad rites for Mr. Brown, who met the deadly reaper yesterday.

5. Most critics agree that there was a method in Hamlet's madness.

6. Already, at sweet sixteen, she was a raving beauty.

7. Last but not least, let me introduce the president of this university.

8. Failing Psychology 101 left me a sadder but wiser budgeter of my time.

9. Off the top of my head, I'd say there are about 400 students in the sophomore class.

10. I was so spaced out yesterday night I didn't hear anything the speaker said.

NAME _____ DATE _____

In the following sentences, underline the trite expressions and replace them with original and interesting phrases.

Example: It was so quiet in the room, you could <u>hear a pin drop.</u>
It was so quiet in the room, you could **hear a mouse sneeze.**

1. When Jim saw the bear, he ran as fast as his legs would carry him.

2. John saw the gigantic bat and turned white as a sheet.

3. You'd better not eat all that cake, unless you want to be fat as a pig.

4. With their courageous ascent of the peak, the climbers covered themselves with glory.

5. It's sad but true that most people procrastinate.

6. When she shook hands with me, her hands were as cold as ice.

7. Having a cousin who is a bank robber has always been the skeleton in the Edwards' closet.

8. That pedigreed chihuahua is the apple of Joe's eye.

9. Marlene said that failing the chemistry test was a fate worse than death.

10. Just a word to the wise, when you're turning in papers, remember—better late than never.

NAME _____ DATE _____

Write five sentences containing phrases that you often
overuse. Rewrite the sentences to eliminate the trite phrases
or replace them with fresher ones.

1.

2.

3.

4.

5.

NAME _____ DATE _____

The following passage has many problems with style. Rewrite the passage to eliminate wrong words, faulty predication, imprecise and inappropriate words, misuse of idiomatic expressions, and trite expressions. It may be necessary to restructure some of the sentences in order to correct them.

Debbie and Steve pinched their pennies in order for buying a house. Talking to realtors and looking at houses was an interesting experience. Some houses had been apprised at an affordable price, but the surrounding neighborhoods were too scuzzy; where the neighborhood was nice, most of the houses were priced sky-high. Debbie and Steve were becoming dejected of not finding an appropriate domicile. Then, they ran over the house of their dreams: a charming little bugaboo on a tree-lined street.

Debbie and Steve were incredulously lucky to find this house. Although it was old, its basic stricture was stolid. The biggest problems were an overgrown back yard and a new exterior paint job. But Debbie and Steve were not put up by the prospect of hard work, since buying an old house is when you get a chance to roll up your sleeves and get down to work.

Among themselves, Debbie and Steve did all the repairs; they worked like beavers all summer. Steve cleared away several popular trees which obfuscated the sunshine, cut back the weeds which ran rampant through the yard, and embedded some interesting horticultural specimens. On account of because Steve got the whirlies when confronted from excessive altitudes, Debbie painted the house. She went to the hardware store to get a chart of suggestive colors, from which she chose a blatant yellow for the shingles and a nice brown for the shutters, verandah, and other extra stuff.

After tremendous efforts, the house was ready. One of the first things of which Debbie and Steve planned to do was to have a housebreaking party. They invited all their friends and consanguineous associates. Everyone agreed that the house was as pretty as a picture, and that Debbie and Steve should be proud for what they had accomplished. Indeed they were—the reason is because it was a good feeling to turn a diamond in the rough into a polished gem.

Style

ITEM 45

AWKWARD SENTENCES

Although they may be grammatically correct, awkward sentences are clumsy and difficult to understand. They generally result from one or more of three types of fault: a) irregular word order, b) wordy or rambling constructions, c) successions of rhyming words. Reading a sentence aloud can often help you identify awkward constructions.

1 Irregular word order

Words and phrases should appear in a sentence in an order that is readily understood and that sounds natural to a native English speaker. Do not needlessly separate modifiers from the words they modify or split phrases that form a unit of thought in a sentence.

Almost, in the accident, John was killed.

Rewrite:
John was almost killed in the accident.

Dr. Jones always has time for, no matter how busy she may be, students who want to see her.

Rewrite:
No matter how busy she may be, Dr. Jones always has time for students who want to see her.

2   Rambling or wordy structures

A rambling sentence contains long strings of phrases and clauses or uses more words than necessary to convey an idea clearly. Since this excess material distracts from the main idea of the sentence, it is best to eliminate unnecessary words and phrases and to form two or more sentences from one long, rambling sentence.

> As I was walking home, I met my aunt in front of Jones' Grocery, which is the best place in town to buy cheese because they have all different kinds of foreign and domestic cheeses at reasonable prices.

Rewrite:
> As I was walking home, I met my aunt in front of Jones' Grocery. That is the best place in town to buy cheese because they have all different kinds of foreign and domestic cheeses at reasonable prices.

3   Unintentional rhyme

If a sentence contains several words that rhyme, those words will stand out because of their sound and will distract attention from the idea the sentence is expressing. Replace rhyming words with synonyms that do not rhyme.

> We could do **away** with the refuse problem in the **bay today,** if the citizens would **say** "yes" to bond issue 53.

Rewrite:
> We could eliminate the refuse problem in the bay immediately, if the citizens would only vote "yes" to bond issue 53.

Rewrite the following sentences to correct irregular word order.

1. To study on the lawn or under the trees, the children left, whenever they wanted to, their schoolroom.

2. We walked down the path slowly bordered by tall firs.

3. She expects to, even though it will be difficult, in three years complete her college course.

4. Almost, they were ready to, when we came, go with us.

5. Very few, only those of grammar and spelling, rules apply to news writing.

6. The last thing a hiker wants to do is to late at night run into on a dark trail a porcupine.

7. Mary was three times elected class president in a row.

8. Nobody got, fortunately, left behind in our group of fifteen or lost.

9. Here we, where the most famous musicians had performed, were in a lovely concert hall, singing.

10. Employees of the firm can only park their cars in this lot.

Rewrite the following rambling sentences so that they are clear and coherent.

1. Around my home town there are ranges of hills like those in West Virginia where I spent a vacation once on my grandfather's farm when I was twelve.

2. Dental hygiene, which is a comparatively new field, offers good jobs at a time when jobs are hard to find, so schools that offer courses in dental hygiene are attracting many students.

3. The art of consistent and impassioned argument without personal animosity or belligerence between the opponents is not practiced in the United States, although one often reads about such arguments in contemporary Russian and French novels, and probably those books offer a fairly reliable picture of the social practices in Russia and France, so we must ask ourselves why such arguments do not exist in our country.

4. Because they left the house hastily, they were drenched to the skin because they had left their raincoats behind even though the sky was cloudy and threatened rain.

5. Having a large family was a helpful experience for my cousin because she became a teacher and could deal with children well because she was used to small children and what they needed.

6. My cousin Jean received an invitation three weeks after returning home from a tour of South America, to visit relatives in Kyoto, Japan, who had been living there for several years and who had wanted her to visit before, but she could never find the time.

7. Only last semester, I took a course in computer programming which I thought would be very helpful for my future career in business, which I enjoyed so much that I'm planning now to change my major to computer science.

8. The long trips across the scorching plains, when food often ran out and people had nothing to eat but what little meat they were able to shoot and when there was constant danger from Indian attacks or sudden storms, were grueling experiences for the pioneers who had set out so eagerly for Oregon, unaware of what lay before them.

9. Mark has been keeping a journal for five years that he writes in every day without fail so that he can look back on these years and remember how it felt to be twenty-five when he is an old man and compare his experiences to those of the young people he will know then.

10. I threw down my pen and dashed out of the house just in time to see the firetruck race by followed by an ambulance and four police cars, all heading up toward the old brick schoolhouse which I was told later had been set on fire by students in their pottery class firing the kiln.

NAME _____ DATE _____

Rewrite the following sentences, underlining awkward rhyming words and replacing them with well-chosen synonyms.

1. I'm amazed at how well her ways of raising rabbits pay.

2. A soft breeze eased through the trees and teased the waters of the pond into ripples.

3. Mr. Hawkins became sage in his old age and seldom flew into the rages he had engaged in when he was younger.

4. For prose writers, my advice is to be concise, use precise language, and avoid the device of rhyme.

5. A closed mind reviews few new ideas.

6. These days, it's difficult to guess who will achieve success.

7. Today was so gloomy and grey I decided to stay in bed.

8. This fall we're all going to play basketball.

9. Alan shouted, "Look out! The tree's about to fall!"

10. We were too late to meet Alice, so we came straight back without waiting.

Style

ITEMS 46 and 47

WORDINESS

---

1   Wordy sentences

Avoid using more words than are necessary to express your ideas; instead, be as direct and concise as possible. A few *well-chosen* and *precise* words are clearer and more effective than long strings of words that add nothing to the meaning of your sentence. Sentences full of jargon are often good examples of wordiness. There are two main ways to correct wordy sentences: by omitting all unnecessary words and by restructuring the sentence.

> The winter snowstorms that occurred in the state of Ohio in the year of 1940 were the worst snowstorms ever recorded in that state.

Rewrite:
> The snowstorms that occurred in Ohio in 1940 were the worst ever recorded in that state.

> Life for the first settlers in the new country held many hardships and privations unknown to those people before they set out from their old homeland.

Rewrite:
> The first settlers in the new country experienced many hardships and privations unknown to them before.

The most effective examples of parental role models can be found in those who maximize both the nurturing and affective elements within the child/parent relationship and the time frames for actual parent/child contact and interaction.

Rewrite:

The best parents are those who spend a great deal of time with their children and show them lots of affection and concern.

---

2   Redundancy

Redundancy is a specific kind of wordiness, occurring when the same or similar words are repeated unnecessarily.

Her coat is red in color.

(Since **red** is a color, the final phrase is unnecessary; it adds nothing to the sentence.)

In the winter in December, the garden plants are quite dead and have to be uprooted and pulled out of the ground.

(**In the winter** and **pulled out of the ground** are unnecessary repetitions of idea. **Dead** is an absolute word that does not need to be intensified.)

NAME _____ DATE _____

Cross out all unnecessary words in the following sentences.

1. In my own opinion, I think that feeding the world's population is very crucial to world peace in our present world of today.

2. Jim's hair is red in color; he is 5'9" in height, and he weighs 180 pounds.

3. In the past, people of one hundred years ago did not have readily available to them the variety of different kinds of food and things to eat that we now find on the supermarket shelves these days.

4. In the year of 1956, I returned back for a visit to my home town where I was born.

5. All the entire day we spent walking on the hills back behind the town; when at last we finally got home, we decided perhaps we had been quite overzealous in our activity of walking.

6. I discovered the cat, which I found sleeping peacefully 6' up overhead in a scraggly pine tree.

7. This newly re-covered couch has recently been reupholstered in a wool fabric.

8. In the spring of the year, many people yearn to travel and take trips away from home.

9. In some classes, students may be physically present in body but mentally absent in spirit.

10. A bright, sunny windowsill is a very ideal spot for growing geraniums.

NAME _____ DATE _____

Correct the wordiness of the following sentences by restructuring them. Do *not* change the basic idea of the sentence.

Example: In his career in a real estate office as a realtor, my brother was never very successful or happy, but he was much more successful and happy when he became a carpenter building houses instead of selling them.

Rewrite: My brother was much happier and more successful as a carpenter than as a realtor—building houses rather than selling them.

1. My cats, who live with me in my house, often cannot be found, for they know every dark corner and all the small, secret places in the house where they can hide.

2. While young people are going through their early adolescence, they sometimes want to experience the security of childhood, but, at the same time, they want to demonstrate adult initiative and responsibility, too.

3. After we left the state of Colorado, we entered the state of Kansas, and from there on we saw only plains, broad rivers, and low hills; the mountains of Colorado were behind us.

4. Now, especially, it is true that this state needs new leadership in the government and not just new leadership, but good new leadership in both the legislature and the governorship.

5. Paul and Virginia found that traveling all over the world could become routine after a few months and they were both matter-of-fact about what had at first been an exciting adventure for them both.

6. First and foremost, every person, as a human being, whether child, adolescent, or adult, has the ability to change his or her life, choosing and directing a new course of life as it progresses through his or her lifetime.

7. One major purpose of education concerns not just the lone individual but society as a whole; this purpose is to produce responsible citizens who can be depended upon to help create an informed, reliable electorate for voting on social issues and concerns.

8. An efficient plant food production unit for a family of six individuals will generally measure 20′ × 30′ in size and will be situated near enough to the family dwelling space to provide convenient access.

9. At times Jean declares to me that she is going to quit attending school and run away to the country of Tahiti; occasionally I make the same comment to her about my own intentions.

10. We were all of us extremely elated at our opportunity actually to visit countries we had previously studied in history classes but which, at the time, we had never really dreamed of visiting, except in our daydreams and fantasies.

Using both methods of correcting wordiness, rewrite the following paragraph on your own paper.

In Homer's epic poem the *Iliad,* the form of a warrior-goddess is the one the goddess Athene most often assumes. She appears stern and terrible; her figure strikes fear, awe, and fright into the hearts of the soldiers. She only has to walk into the Achean camp to rouse the soldiers to fierce fighting mettle. Her battle cry terrifies her enemies very much. In this fierce side of her nature, however, there exists in her no brutality or excessive bloodthirstiness, even though she is a fierce warrior. Instead, she is like a general in an army who is implacable in battle, fighting fiercely, yet cool-headed, well versed in strategy, who knows how best to use an army to the best advantage. Athene knows, too, when there is also a time for peace. Thus, she guides the spear of Diomedes against Pandaros and gives Diomedes great prowess in battle by her aid in the fight; she wounds a sister goddess Aphrodite in her fury, but she also counsels with Apollo for an armistice to stop the fighting, and she stops Ares in his quite rash scheme to avenge his son by taking fierce revenge on his son's slayers. Athene is a terrible figure as a warrior-goddess in war, but she is also prudent and a strategist, as mentioned before. In warfare, she knows when to stop fighting.

Style

MIXED METAPHOR

Metaphor is based on comparison; similar qualities are seen in two different things. Mixed metaphors occur when the objects of comparison are joined incongruously or inconsistently. Often this is a result of writing in clichés rather than creating fresh images.

> A person sets out in life on a sea of possibilities, **only to strike out immediately**.

Rewrite:
> A person sets out in life on a sea of possibilities, **only to suffer immediate shipwreck in some storm**.

It is inconsistent to speak of a sea voyage in terms of baseball. The rewritten sentence shows the consistent metaphor of personal experience compared to a sea voyage.

Replace the mixed metaphors in the following sentences with clear, consistent metaphors.

Example: In the debate, Jim put all his cards on the table, but his opponent threw him a curve.

In the debate, Jim put all his cards on the table, but his opponent **had an ace up his sleeve**.

1. The disease of jealousy had already stabbed him in the back.

2. It's an uphill climb, trying to keep our balance on the narrow bridge of economic stability.

3. By the time Mark was twenty, he had achieved the pinnacle of success, only to find it was a pig in a poke.

4. His words sprang into her mind like lions and nestled in her heart.

5. The old man had come into safe harbor at last, after leaping all the barriers life had placed before him.

6. My history professor is a regular gold mine of information; he's always bringing up new pearls of wisdom for the class.

7. When he gets a new bee in his bonnet, he never takes time to weigh its results in the balance.

8. We expect our new survey to take the public pulse at the grass roots of society.

9. The manager streaks across the office every morning like a meteor and invades the conference room.

10. The cancer of apathy can drown our lives if we aren't constantly vigilant.

Circle the letter of the best completion for each of the following metaphoric statements.

Example: My love is a diamond
     a. that warms my heart.
     ⓑ in whose facets I see all the world reflected.
     c. and my heart the oyster that encloses it.

1. It's better not to wait for opportunity to knock at your door;
     a. you should jump on the bandwagon yourself.
     b. go out to meet it on the road.
     c. grab it on the wing.

2. His anger stormed through his neighbor's arguments
     a. and ricocheted from the wall of his prejudice.
     b. and drowned in his prejudice.
     c. and beat against a solid wall of prejudice.

3. Hope is a faint star
     a. that makes its nest in our hearts.
     b. that leads us when our souls are dark.
     c. with deep roots in our souls.

4. Ideas planted in careful thought
     a. will not easily be uprooted by the passing winds of popular opinion.
     b. will not easily catch fire from the sparks of popular opinion.
     c. will not be blinded by the glare of popular opinion.

5. I just skated through that exam
     a. and cleared all the bases.
     b. even over the thin ice.
     c. without hitting a single false note.

6. My anger grew like a weed
   a. in the prison of my silence.
   b. in the fertile soil of my silence.
   c. and leaped the walls of my silence.

7. Weigh your actions carefully
   a. before you plunge into decision.
   b. so you won't be left holding the ball.
   c. before you tip the scales with a decision.

8. My daydream flowed on, taking a leisurely, winding course
   a. until it was roughly broken off.
   b. until it ran up against a stone wall.
   c. until it emptied into sleep.

9. This semester my instructors have rained tests on me
   a. until my mind feels completely waterlogged.
   b. until all my ideas have just dried up.
   c. until I just feel drugged.

10. The setting sun flamed through the clouds for a moment
   a. before darkness smothered it.
   b. before darkness devoured it.
   c. before darkness crept over it.

Compose five sentences containing original and consistent metaphors.

1.

2.

3.

4.

5.

Style

ITEM 49

USE OF ACTIVE AND PASSIVE VOICE

Choice of an active or a passive verb can influence the effect or tone of a sentence. As the names indicate, **active** voice emphasizes the action of the sentence and its performer; **passive** voice emphasizes the receiver of the action. Generally, active verbs are more forceful and direct than passive verbs.

Active Voice: In the beginning, God created the heavens and the earth.
Passive Voice: In the beginning, the heavens and the earth were created by God.

If the receiver of the action is more important than the actor, passive voice is the most effective choice to make.

Mary is loved by everyone who knows her.

(Here the emphasis is on Mary rather than on the people who know her.)

The passive voice can also suggest detachment or objectivity. Scientific writing often makes use of passive verb forms.

My conclusions have been based on data from 406 separate experiments.

Too much use of the passive voice, however, will tend to make your writing tedious and colorless.

Avoid unnecessary switching from one voice to another; this switching is confusing and awkward.

Jim and I stayed home all day, and **many of our chores were finished**.

Rewrite:
Jim and I stayed home all day and **finished many of our chores**.

Decide whether or not the passive voice has been used effectively in the following sentences. Write *E* after the effective sentences. Rewrite ineffective sentences in the active voice.

1. The child was snatched up by its father and carried out of the street.

2. The three businessmen ran wildly down the street, but the bus was missed.

3. A salt is formed by the combination of an acid with a base.

4. The chasm was leaped by the escaping bandit.

5. His house can easily be missed by passers-by; it's a long way back from the road.

6. Safety should be considered before speed.

7. The peas, tomatoes, beets, and squash were grown by me.

8. William Carter was elected mayor by an overwhelming majority.

9. The fox was followed by the hounds, but they lost its scent in the creek.

10. Help! We've been trapped by an enraged porcupine!

The following paragraph is dull and awkward because of excessive use of the passive voice. Rewrite the paragraph using the active voice wherever possible.

A whole series of characters, distinctly his own, has been created by Turgenev in his novels. Among them are shown numerous figures of women whose vitality is attested by the very fact that it has been, and still is, so strenuously debated. We have been told by one critic that only one type of character was ever developed by Turgenev. But, it is also stated just as strongly by another critic that Turgenev's characters are never types, but realistic individuals. In regard to the women characters, the truth lies somewhere between these two viewpoints. Each woman is made part of a broad category, but within that category, one character could not be substituted for another. It is as though the individual was meant by the author to be just that—individual—yet to convey the emotional impact of a type.

NAME _____ DATE _____

The following passage is awkward and confusing. Revise the passage to eliminate awkward sentences, wordiness, mixed metaphors, and ineffective use of the passive voice. You may need to restructure some of the sentences in order to correct them.

Excited was Tom on his first day of work. Finding a job in today's tight job market of limited employment opportunities had not been easy. Applications were filed by Tom at many companies. Almost, several times Tom was offered a job, only to have his hopes crushed in a sea of disappointment. Still, he continued on with his job-hunting. A job was finally gotten as a salesman of photocopying equipment and Tom was pleased because this was an industry that was expanding rapidly and had many possibilities of upward mobility for a young salesman to advance forward which made him very happy.

Tom set out to find out all about the ins and outs of his new job. The qualities of perseverance, initiative, and friendliness were needed by anyone who hoped to succeed at sales. The industry was a competitive dog-eat-dog rat race. To Tom, it was clear that if he was going to succeed and amount to anything at all in this business he would have to put his nose to the grindstone and burn the midnight oil until the well ran dry. That he was ambitious and energetic was obvious to anyone with whom he worked which proved to be of great help in achieving eventual success.

By the end of the first month, the consensus of opinion was that Tom had the potential to eventually master the essentials of the job and become especially important to the future of the company. Over $200,000 of equipment was sold by Tom during that first month.

Particularly, Tom was pleased to have sold a complete system to Mr. Forest who was the owner of a large sporting goods factory which employed thousands of people and was the largest employer in town, as a result of which Mr. Forest was pursued by many salesmen. The true fact of the matter was that Mr. Forest was an impervious tower of indifference, but Tom rose to the challenge and burrowed through it. This was a very unique situation for a young salesman. Tom was rewarded for his efforts by his manager with a Salesman of the Month award.

Paragraphing

ITEM 50

UNITY IN THE PARAGRAPH

The paragraph is a group of sentences developing a single main topic, which will often be stated in a topic sentence. Every sentence in the paragraph should contribute to the development of that central idea. If all ideas in a paragraph are carefully related to the topic, the paragraph will be unified.

1   Clear, Definite Topic Sentences

Unity of the paragraph begins with a clear, definite topic sentence which is often a general statement that will be specified and supported in the rest of the paragraph. This sentence should state *exactly* what will be discussed in the paragraph.

In Greek mythology, Athene often appears as a warrior-goddess, stern and terrifying.

This sentence states clearly and definitely the aspects of Athene that will be discussed in the paragraph. No other aspects of the goddess besides her connection with war and her stern, terrifying nature will be relevant to the paragraph.

Since the topic sentence also serves to *limit* and *define* the paragraph's main idea, it is important to state topic sentences as specifically as possible.

Paragraphs written on vague or overgeneralized topics will be confusing and dull, both for you and for your reader.

Swimming is good for people.

Rewrite:

Swimming can provide good physical therapy for handicapped people.

The first sentence would not make a good topic sentence. Swimming might be good for various types of people—children, the handicapped, weight-watchers—in a number of different ways. You could not discuss all of these aspects of your subject in one paragraph. To present a subject that could be covered adequately in one paragraph, you need to narrow and specify the topic sentence.

The topic sentence may or may not actually appear in the finished paragraph, but it must *always* be present in the mind of the writer. It is a good idea for beginning writers to always include topic sentences in their paragraphs to avoid confusion.

2 Developing Topic Sentences

All other sentences in a paragraph will develop the idea of the topic sentence. Nothing should be allowed into the paragraph that is unnecessary or irrelevant to that idea.

Identify and underline the vague or unclear parts of the following sentences and rewrite them so that they could be used as topic sentences for paragraphs.

Example: Abraham Lincoln was <u>an important man</u>.
             (The underlined phrase is vague and undefined.)

Rewrite:

Abraham Lincoln brought a sense of integrity and purpose to the presidency at a time when the nation was seriously divided.
(This revision specifies ways in which Lincoln was important. Other definite topic sentences might be composed that state why Lincoln was important.)

1. Comparing a country-western song with a hard-rock song, I find that the country-western song has more meaning than the hard-rock song.

2. People in our culture have ideas and beliefs that are different from those of another culture.

3. The book *The Heart of the Matter* was interesting only in some parts.

4. Television affects people.

5. Energy is a problem.

6. There are many aspects to student evaluations.

7. Life is hard.

8. Today's education isn't working.

9. Returning students often have a hard time.

10. Every human being is a curious mixture.

Identify and underline the topic sentence in each of the following paragraphs.

1. Game and sport fish are among the most carefully tended and conserved of all natural resources, but the rest of our native fishes receive virtually no attention, and a number have become extinct in recent years or are in danger of extinction. This is especially true of the fresh-water fishes of the southwestern United States, where there is hardly a river or stream that has not been affected by the activities of man. Because aquatic habitats in the desert are isolated for long periods of time, punctuated infrequently by floods, the distribution pattern of the fishes of the Southwest once provided an exceptional opportunity for the study of speciation and zoogeography. Now the pattern has been thoroughly disrupted, often unnecessarily, and if anything like it still exists in the world, it is not in North America.

(David W. Ehrenfeld, *Biological Conservation*)

2. The human race, as it immediately concerns us, has a vertical axis of about 40,000 years and as of 1900 A.D. a horizontal spread of roughly 3000 different languages and 1000 different cultures. Every living culture and language is the result of countless cross-fertilizations—not a "rise and fall" of civilizations, but more like a flower-like periodic absorbing-blooming-bursting and scattering of seed. Today we are aware as never before of the plurality of human life-styles and possibilities, while at the same time being tied, like in an old silent movie, to a runaway locomotive rushing headlong toward a very singular catastrophe. Science, as far as it is capable of looking "on beauty bare," is on our side. Part of our being modern is the very fact of our awareness that we are one with our beginnings—contemporary with all periods—members of all cultures. The seeds of every social structure or custom are in the mind.

(Gary Snyder, *Earth House Hold*)

3. In such a day, in September or October, Walden is a perfect forest mirror, set round with stones as precious to my eye if fewer or rarer. Nothing so fair, so pure, and at the same time so large, as a lake, perchance, lies on the surface of the earth. Sky water. It needs no fence. Nations come and go without defiling it. It is a mirror which no stone can crack, whose quicksilver will never wear off, whose gilding Nature continually repairs; no storms, no dust, can dim its surface ever fresh;—a mirror in which all impurity presented to it sinks, swept and dusted by the sun's hazy brush,—this the light dust-cloth,—which retains no breath that is breathed on it, but sends its own to float as clouds high above its surface, and be reflected in its bosom still.

(H. D. Thoreau, *Walden*)

4. Where the irrigating ditches are shallow and a little neglected, they choke quickly with watercress that multiplies about the lowest Sierra springs. It is characteristic of the frequenters of water borders near man haunts, that they are chiefly of the sorts that are useful to man, as if they made their services an excuse for the intrusion. The joint-grass of soggy pastures produces edible, nut-flavored tubers, called by the Indians *taboose*. The common reed of the ultramontane marshes (here *Phragmites vulgaris*), a very stately, whispering reed, light and strong for shafts or arrows, affords sweet sap and pith which makes a passable sugar.

(Mary Austin, *The Land of Little Rain*)

5. When two continental masses happen to move on a collision course, they gradually close out the sea between them—barging over trenches, shutting them off—and when they hit they drive their leading edges together as a high and sutured welt, resulting in a new and larger continental mass. The Urals are such a welt. So is the Himalaya. The Himalaya is the crowning achievement of the vigorous Australian Plate, of which India is the northernmost extremity. India in the Oligocene, completing its long northward journey, crashed head on into Tibet, hit so hard that it not only folded and buckled the plate boundaries but also plowed in under the newly created Tibetan plateau and drove the Himalaya five and a half miles up into the sky. The mountains are in some trouble. India has not stopped pushing them, and they are still going up. Their height and volume are already so great they are beginning to melt in their own self-generated radioactive heat. When the climbers in 1953 planted their flags on the highest mountain, they set them in snow over the skeletons of creatures that had lived in the warm clear ocean that India, moving north, blanked out. Possibly as much as twenty thousand feet below the seafloor, the skeletal remains had formed into rock. This one fact is a treatise in itself on the movements of the surface of the earth. If by some fiat I had to restrict all this writing to one sentence, this is the one I would choose: The summit of Mt. Everest is marine limestone.

(John McPhee, *Basin and Range*)

No topic statements appear in the following paragraphs. Compose a topic sentence for each of them, expressing the main idea of the paragraph.

1. You may see from a boat, in calm weather, near the sandy eastern shore, where the water is eight or ten feet deep, and also in some other parts of the pond, circular heaps half a dozen feet in diameter by a foot in height, consisting of small stones less than a hen's egg in size where all around is bare sand. At first you wonder if the Indians could have formed them on the ice for any purpose, and so, when the ice melted, they sank to the bottom; but they are too regular and some of them plainly too fresh for that. They are similar to those found in rivers; but as there are no suckers nor lampreys here, I know not by what fish they could be made. Perhaps they are the nests of the chivin. These lend a pleasing mystery to the bottom.

(H. D. Thoreau, *Walden*)

2. Ten minutes into our morning watch we spotted a finback; he spouted six times at intervals of six to ten seconds; sounded, and was gone. Not until 6:30 P.M. was our day's patience rewarded. Forty or fifty white-sided dolphins, three-quarters of a mile to the west, were soaring and cavorting in the fading light of the evening. In a line nearly a quarter of a mile long, they were strung out, seven-to-nine foot dolphins leaping as high as twice their body length out of the water, twisting, swirling, and whirling with exuberance. Within moments of spotting them, we were joined by Stanley, Richard, and the Chief, who were beginning to feel the magic too.

(Gordon S. Hayward, "A Whalewatcher's Diary," *Country Journal*, August 1977)

3. The migrant worker gets up at five A.M., is picked up in a roadside barrio at six A.M. and loaded into a bus, truck, or van with other workers. He is driven five, ten, or thirty miles to the fields to work the day under a hot sun. A break in the midmorning, thirty minutes for lunch, and a ten-minute break in the afternoon provide his only rest periods. He spends the rest of the day either hunched down cutting lettuce, carrying a ladder from one orange tree to another, or picking grapes from the vines. After a ten-hour workday, he is taken back to his desolate barrio.

(James Santibanez, "El Teatro Campesino Today and El Teatro Urbano," *The Chicano*)

4. Now an old brown log is glorified with the evening sun-glow. Two bars of mellow light shoot up the meadow; both margins are in shadow, with scarce a flower panicle stirring in the hush. Here and there a willow-tuft glows against the gray shade. One grand promontory of firs stands full in the light, the long branches clad in yellow lichen. Farther back the brown trunks are flecked with sunshine, and on the north side one young pine towers transfigured, while all its companions are in shadow.

(John Muir, *John of the Mountains,* ed. Linnie Marsh Wolfe)

5. Alighting to a depth of four inches or more, the grasshoppers covered every inch of ground, every plant and shrub. Tree limbs snapped under their weight, corn stalks bent to the ground, potato vines were mashed flat. Quickly and cleanly, these voracious pests devoured everything in their paths. No living plant could escape. Whole fields of wheat, corn and vegetables disappeared; trees and shrubs were completely denuded. Even turnips, tobacco and tansy vanished.

(Joanna L. Stratton, *Pioneer Women*)

On your own paper, rewrite the following paragraphs so that all the sentences relate to the topic statement. Omit unnecessary statements; add anything that you think is needed to make a unified and complete paragraph.

1. This story was interesting, only in some parts. The parts I really enjoyed were some of the poems; for example, there was a poem on page 296. This story was about Wilson and some other characters. Wilson seemed to like poetry, and he absorbed it secretly like a drug. He never had a car of his own. He felt almost intolerably lonely. He also seemed to talk a lot about Scobie. Scobie was still a novice in the world of deceit; so was Wilson. He hadn't lived in it since childhood, and he felt an odd elderly envy for Scobie, much as an old crook might envy the young crook serving his first sentence to whom all this was new. I also enjoyed the part where they found the diary.

2. Utah is a land of strong contrasts. Forested mountains in the north give way to salt plains, harsh deserts adjoin fertile farm lands, miles of sparsely populated country surround the metropolitan area of Salt Lake City. Perhaps Utah is best known to the traveler for its fruit orchards. In the spring, the countryside is filled with flowering trees. Both the Green River and the Colorado River flow through the state, the one winding down from high Wyoming mountains, the other entering Utah across the western Colorado prairie. These great rivers cut through the southern sandstone desert, forming corridors of vegetation in an arid country. People who tried to navigate these rivers often perished. Salt Lake City is the capital of Utah. It is an industrial center with its steel mills and oil refineries, lying between the mountains on the east and the Great Salt Lake. But agriculture is also a basic part of Utah's economy. The pioneers must have admired this valley, for their first settlement was here. Utah is called the Beehive State.

3. It was hard for my father and mother to accept our decision to move. At first, they felt we were abandoning them just at the time in their lives when they needed support. My father is 75 and my mother, 73; thus, they worried about illness or inability to get around town without us there to help. My father has only really been sick once in his life, however. On the other hand, my mother has had pneumonia three times; once she almost died from it. They also worried that we would be so far away from them that they would lose touch with our lives, maybe even our affections. One of my mother's friends has a daughter who lives in Milwaukee, and she never writes, but she hardly saw her mother even when they were both living in the same town. And finally, my father was somewhat hurt that we were leaving the family business to work for another, larger company.

4. When you begin to hunt for an apartment, the most important thing to keep in mind is how well the owner maintains the property. I've seen some terribly run-down apartments over the years; it makes me wonder how people can be so careless about their rentals. Look first at the apartment building's general appearance. Is it tidy and neat? Are all the windows intact? Does the porch sag? People have been seriously injured when porch roofs collapsed on them. Inside, look for water stains on ceilings and walls that might indicate a leaky roof. Sometimes I have lain awake at night, staring at the shapes watermarks made on the ceiling; they often look like strange monsters. The inside walls should also be fairly recently painted and clean with no large cracks or gaps in them. Just looking for these sorts of signs can tell you a lot about the apartment's condition as well as how much interest the owner takes in the property. Some landlords don't care what you do. You could have a St. Bernard dog in a three-room apartment, and they wouldn't complain.

5. At certain times in my life, I have found myself reflecting on my lifestyle and circumstances and deciding whether my life satisfied me. Just a year ago, I went through one of those periods. I was a successful market analyst, convinced of the importance of my responsibilities and enjoying the work I performed. My boss was fine, too, never getting angry over small details or expecting miracles from my department. But somehow, I felt dissatisfied with my life. Thinking about the ways I spent my time, I discovered that there was very little in my life beyond my work, a few parties with friends, and the usual household chores everyone faces. I have a small apartment, so there isn't a lot to do. Still, there are always dishes to wash and the weekly dusting and sweeping. Actually, I'm a fairly tidy person, so I never have a *real* mess to worry about. Still, I realized then that I was not deriving enough personal satisfaction from my work or my relaxation. I did not feel I was growing intellectually or being challenged to learn new skills. I've always wanted to learn Spanish, but I never seem to find the time. And I'd love to be able to paint, though I might not be very good at it.

Choose one of the rewritten topics from Exercise 1 and write your own clear, unified paragraph. The topic sentence should appear somewhere in your paragraph.

Paragraphing

ITEM 51

COHERENCE IN THE PARAGRAPH

1 Coherence in the Paragraph

Coherence in the paragraph means that the sentences are written, arranged, and interlinked so that the thought introduced in the first sentence develops smoothly and clearly from one sentence to the next. The reader should be able to follow the development of an idea easily and logically, without confusion about the relationship of each sentence to those preceding and following it.

2 Main methods of achieving paragraph coherence

There are two main methods of achieving paragraph coherence:

a. Sentence arrangement. The sentences of the paragraph should be arranged so that each is related to the one that comes before and the one that comes after. This arrangement may be temporal, spatial, or logical (following a pattern such as cause and effect, inductive use of detail to support a general statement, etc.). Parallel sentence structure is also a method of achieving coherence.

b. Transitional words. Transitional or connective words are words that connect the thought of one sentence to that of preceding sentences. These linking words are such words as pronouns, demonstrative adjectives (**this**, **that**, **these**, **those**), conjunctions, or conjunctive adverbs (**however**, **moreover**, **also**, **hence**, and so on).

Most often, both of these methods are used together to give coherence to a paragraph, although either may be used separately.

Example: Stepping carefully around the straggling prickly pear I come after a few paces over bare sandstone to a plant whose defensive weaponry makes the cactus seem relatively benign. **This one** is formed of a cluster of bayonetlike leaves pointing up and outward, each stiff green blade tipped with a point as intense and penetrating as a needle. Out of the core of **this untouchable dagger's nest** rises a slender stalk, waist-high, gracefully curved, which supports a heavy cluster of bell-shaped, cream-colored, wax-coated, exquisitely perfumed flowers. **This plant,** not a cactus but a member of the lily family, is a type of yucca called Spanish bayonet.

(Edward Abbey, *Desert Solitaire*)

This paragraph employs complementary spatial and logical patterns of organization. Spatial sequence shows the plant's surroundings first, then its leaves, stalk, and finally its most beautiful part, the flowers; this sequence follows the writer's eye as he looks at the plant. The logical sequence begins with an assertion that the plant's leaves are *defensive weaponry* and continues with a description of the defenses. The writer then reveals what is being defended (the *purpose* of the formidable leaves). The final sentence identifies the plant for the reader. Notice the repetition of words similar to the plant's name, *bayonetlike, dagger's nest,* and also the frequent use of the demonstrative adjective *this.*

Example: Many a skier drives forward, but, as his legs pass each other, he relaxes and discontinues the knee-drive. There is not as much power or extension **there**, and **such skiers** will not go so fast. **This kind of skiing** is often telegraphed by the arm movements or body position. If the body is upright, chances are the forward knee-drive is insufficient. If the arms come forward with elbows bent sharply or don't go backward beyond the hip, their shortened swing is proof that the extension is not complete.

(John Caldwell, *The New Cross-Country Ski Book*)

This paragraph's organization is based on a kind of cause-and-effect structure. A type of faulty skiing technique is introduced in the first sentence. The second sentence shows the effects of this technique on performance. The final three sentences illustrate the physical effects of such skiing which are external signs of the skier's mistakes. The last two sentences are parallel in structure, a sophisticated method of keeping the paragraph coherent. The transitional words appear in boldface.

Decide whether or not the following paragraphs are coherent. If they are, write *coherent* in the space provided; if they are not, write *incoherent*.

1. Students on today's campuses have often been called apathetic; they seem to do nothing, to be interested in very little. But often the so-called apathy is simply the result of fear, whether fear of failure, disapproval, or commitment to a new set of ideas. The real problem of student apathy, then, lies in the inability of students, faculty, and administration alike to find ways in which to lessen that fear, to assure that curiosity and investigation need not be penalized. Such exploration in itself might be considered a worthy undertaking, apart from the usual categories of success and failure. _____

2. A football coach's job isn't as simple as it may sound. Games are won, not only on the field, but during long training sessions. Many college football players go on to become professionals. These men need many talents. The coach must find his players' strengths and use them efficiently. After training sessions, the team's weaknesses and strengths are analyzed by the coach and this is when he must make his key decisions. A good coach is a strategist, analyst, teacher, and psychologist. He must also discover the opposing team's weak points and try to make use of them in planning his own team's game. _____

3. More and more people these days are adopting a vegetarian diet. Many people simply feel they do not wish to contribute to the slaughter of animals. There are various types of vegetarianism. Most vegetarians exclude all meat and fish from their diet; others, however, are stricter. They exclude dairy products and eggs as well as meat. One point in favor of vegetarianism is that a vegetable diet is often less expensive than a meat-based diet. There seem to be no ill effects from a vegetarian diet if it is carefully balanced nutritionally. Some vegetarians even expand their diet to include fish and sea foods. Also, vegetarians contend that more people can be fed on a vegetable-based agriculture than on a meat-based one. _____

4. About five years ago I met one of the most remarkable women I've ever known. She had just been appointed librarian of the Tarsville Public Library, her name was May Gibbons, and she was seventy years old. What led her, at her age, to become librarian for such a small town was her strong conviction that people should read and that books should be available to everyone. From her first day on the job, she was untiring. She solicited money from the City Council for library funds, collected books, instituted reading programs for children, and widely publicized the town's "new" library. This enthusiasm has been contagious, and the Tarsville Public Library is now a center of the town's life. And, of course, at the center of the library's success is May Gibbons. _____

5. During the first few days at a university, a student must make many difficult adjustments. The new student must adjust to cafeteria hours and cooking. Living with a roommate instead of a familiar brother or sister can mean adjusting to new demands on one's time or to new lifestyles. These problems of living with a stranger are augmented for the freshman who has always had a private room at home. Then, there are books to buy, classes to find, and a whole new schedule to adapt to. But, once the student has overcome these problems, a whole new world is opened for him or her. _____

NAME _____ DATE _____

Read the following sentences carefully and arrange them in the best order to form a coherent paragraph. Explain briefly what clues led you to select your ordering of the sentences.

1. a. No matter how immature it is, it is already as rigid as a mast, with tier on tier of whorled, perfectly horizontal branches that are too short and stiff to bend.
   b. So the foliage instead of being a flat spray, as in the Eastern Balsam Fir, is a spiky bed on which the snowfall is speared and held in cottony tufts.
   c. Some, like the graceful but weaktipped Douglas Firs and the Hemlocks, bend under it, especially while young, till they look like sheeted ghosts all doubled up, or crouching, as if convulsed either with mirth or with pain, but scarcely recognizable as trees.
   d. Many other conifers have flexible needles, but those of this Fir are at once stiff and all, as it were, brushed upward to the top of the twig.
   e. If it is to escape these leafy fingers it will have to melt; the sturdy needles refuse to yield to it and spill it.
   f. Not so the Alpine Fir.
   g. Many kinds of trees that love the mountain heights must for long seasons bear great weights of snow.

   (Donald Culross Peattie, *A Natural History of Western Trees*)

2. a. An oilman who visited the ranch offered him twice his salary to come to Oklahoma and run a ranch that he had there.
   b. He called Buck Peebles, a silent wiry type who hauls cattle and household goods and Mexican shearers and goats and anything else that's willing to ride on his old truck and pay for the privilege.
   c. He was a good foreman and liked his job and liked his boss.
   d. But finally, when the offer got to three times his salary and his wife was shoving at him to think of the kids and even his current employer admitted—wryly—that he wouldn't blame him in the least for going, he agreed.
   e. They loaded on the furniture and the kids and the wife, and drove 200 miles up to the new place.
   f. I knew a cedar-hill man who served as foreman on one of the new cleared ranches built by city men in that region.
   g. He turned it down.

   (John Graves, *Goodbye to a River*)

3. a. The more challenging game animals like deer certainly rank high.
   b. Time after time we have been on field trips with seasoned mountain people who refuse to enter an abandoned house or meadow or cave because it looks so "snakey."
   c. It is difficult to say what variety of mountain wildlife holds the place of honor in fireside conversations.
   d. And of course there are the more dangerous ones like panthers and bears with which nearly every hunter has had his moments of terror.
   e. And time after time we have been amazed at the quality and variety of tales evoked by the mere mention of snakes.
   f. Few living things, however, occupy the place of respect and awe that snakes enjoy.

   ("Snake Lore," *The Foxfire Book*)

4. a. Once every 10,000 years or so they come close to the sun, rapidly traverse the inner portion of their orbits, and then speed back out again to the depths of space.
   b. The "wind" of atoms flowing out from the sun—the extremities of the solar corona—catches comet material and blows it out into a long, luminous tail, sometimes stretching millions of miles in a direction away from the sun.
   c. The solar system has many comets, which probably are huge chunks of loosely packed ices—frozen gases such as carbon dioxide (dry ice), methane, cyanogen, and ammonia, in addition to ordinary water.
   d. During this fleeting visit to the solar neighborhood, the comet encounters sunlight, which melts and evaporates some of the ices.
   e. Comets usually move in highly elliptical orbits, spending most of their time in the frigid regions far beyond the orbits of the giant planets—even beyond Pluto.

   (Donald H. Menzel, *A Field Guide to the Stars and Planets*)

5. a. Nobody stood around in place and gave orders or collected fees; they all simply ran around, picking up pellets at random and dropping them again.
   b. After reaching a certain height, the construction stopped unless another column was being formed nearby; in this case the structure changed from a column to an arch, bending off in a smooth curve, the arch was joined, and the termites then set off to build another.
   c. Then, by chance, two or three pellets happened to light on top of each other, and this transformed the behavior of everyone.
   d. Grasse placed a handful of termites in a dish filled with soil and fecal pellets (these are made of lignin, a sort of micro-lumber) and watched what they did.
   e. Now they displayed the greatest interest and directed their attention obsessively to the primitive column, adding new pellets and fragments of earth.
   f. They did not, in the first place, behave at all like contractors.

   (Lewis Thomas, "Living Language," *The Lives of a Cell*)

Using both methods of achieving paragraph coherence, rewrite those paragraphs from Exercise 1 that you marked *incoherent*. Underline the transitional words that you use.

Paragraphing

ITEM 52

ADEQUATE DEVELOPMENT OF THE PARAGRAPH

Except for special purposes, such as emphasis, transition, or dialogue, every paragraph should be developed in more than one or two sentences. The writer must give enough information in each paragraph to explain or support adequately the topic of that paragraph. Often context will be important in determining how much development a paragraph needs; each paragraph must be seen in relationship to the paragraphs before and after it.

1   **The topic sentence acts as the foundation for a paragraph; it will determine to a large extent how much development the paragraph needs.**

Example: Ever since man first began to travel long distances he has wittingly and unwittingly brought other creatures along with him. The dingo . . . evidently came to the island continent (Australia) as the companion of prehistoric man during the late pleistocene, so transplantation is not new. As the human population increases, and as rapid travel becomes commonplace, nonhuman hitchhikers abound: Insects and spiders accompany bananas; rats, mice and even cats sneak off ships that are loading cargo at remote, oceanic islands; and the American traveler returning from Europe brings back European cold viruses along with new watches, scarves, and ash trays (the European traveler in America does the same). Foreign organisms are spread in other ways. Agricultural animals (like pigs) and plants (like coconuts) escape readily from domestication. People also transport and release animals and plants because they like them or because they like to hunt them or fish for them. Flocks of hundreds of Australian budgerigars (parakeets) wheel over St. Petersburg, Florida, and schools of Coho (Pacific) salmon thrive in lakes Michigan and Superior, where they give joy to fishermen and feed on another recent arrival, the alewife.

(David W. Ehrenfeld, *Biological Conservation*)

The topic sentence of this paragraph (the first sentence) indicates that three aspects of human transmission of animal and plant life will be discussed: that this has taken place over a long period of time, that this has occurred without man's conscious aid, and that this has often been the result of conscious human action. Examples are given to illustrate each of these contentions. If the topic sentence had mentioned **four** aspects of transmission of plant and animal life, the paragraph would not be adequately developed by a discussion of only **three** aspects.

Once a paragraph topic has been introduced, the writer is under an obligation to the reader to make that idea understandable and complete. Enough information should be supplied to answer the reader's main questions about the topic. Often the basis for adequate development of a paragraph will lie in the presentation of specific details about the general topic being discussed.

2   Methods of Development

There are many possible methods for developing paragraphs and providing adequate support for the topic statement. Some of the most often used are these:

A. Supportive detail, including examples, illustrations, facts, statistics, and testimony of other people
(The paragraph in section **1** is developed through supportive detail. Ehrenfeld gives examples of various animals carried long distances by man.)

B. Definition of key terms

C. Comparison or contrast of topic idea or event with an idea or event more familiar to readers

D. Causes and/or effects of topic idea or event

E. Description of topic idea or event

F. Explanation of how topic idea or event operates

Any of these methods of paragraph development may be used in combination as well as separately. The writer's choice among them will be based on which best suits the type of subject discussed in a particular paragraph, the information available to the writer, and the place of the paragraph in the whole essay.

Assume that the following sentences are topic sentences of paragraphs. Indicate for each one what will be discussed in its paragraph. Be as specific as possible.

Example:　　Most of the action in *Return of the Jedi* might have come straight from a standard western.

　　　　　To develop this paragraph, the writer will have to show what the action of a standard western involves—good guys versus bad guys, romance kept to a minimum, constant action, last minute suspense, and so on. Illustrations from *Return of the Jedi* must be given to show that it fits this pattern.

1. Spending a quiet afternoon alone can be a good way to deal with tension and nervousness.

2. Dr. Jones, the pediatrician, perfectly illustrates what a good children's doctor should be.

3. Registration can be a confusing process for the new student.

4. An academic scholarship should be given only to people who meet certain definite standards.

5. In many ways, Atlanta is a typical southern town.

6. Dreams can often be expressions of the dreamer's waking concerns.

7. University life has helped me understand more about myself.

8. One reason people travel is to gain a clearer sense of their own identities.

9. The arrival of spring always seems to affect my emotional condition strongly.

10. The boundary between the arts and the sciences is not always easy to define.

Read the following paragraphs carefully. Write *adequate* after those that have been adequately developed and *inadequate* after those that have not. Explain what methods have been used to develop the adequate paragraphs.

1. Some people like to dance to fast music and other people like to dance only to slow music. All people dance the way they feel they can follow the beat best.

2. Many people feel that cloudy, rainy days are depressing and gloomy. But, actually, there need be no correlation between rainy days and depression. I learned this when I lived on the Pacific coast.

3. In the years that followed its founding, the town grew gradually, attracted more businesses, expanded its boundaries, and offered a greater variety of employment to its citizens. Statehood gave a great stimulus to the development of Ohio towns, and the rate of growth of Milltown quickened. In 1905, the railroad came to Milltown and with the railroad came new ethnic groups, Irish and Chinese. Milltown was on its way to becoming a large, diversely populated city.

4. The country in which I grew up was a land of great variety and beauty. As a child, I often enjoyed the warm, sunny climate and rolling hills. It was a perfect country for a child. I had a wonderful time growing up there.

5. As scouts, we learned to read the information left by the passing of people, animals, and time through the woods. Our teacher was an old man whose very survival had depended on these skills, and he impressed upon us the importance of clear sight and good memory. We learned to recognize different animal signs, to determine whether branches had been broken and rocks dislodged by animals, people, or only wind or water. We learned which plants could be eaten and which were poisonous. We were able, after some practice, to sit quietly and watch the forest animals go about their own business. And we learned to lay and follow trails, often spending whole days leading one another about the woods.

6. The Renaissance ideal of the perfect courtier is perhaps best described as a man whose every action and attitude would be suitable to his position. He would not flaunt his clothes or his abilities in front of others. He would be high-born, restrained, sensitive. His reason would be taught to discipline his whole character. Such a man may be seen in Titian's painting *Man with the Glove,* and Shakespeare could not have created Hamlet without this dignified image of what a noble man should be.

7. A student coming from a small high school may often feel lonely and frightened at first at a large university. Most of the people are strangers. The new student feels anonymous and insignificant. He is lost in a world not his own.

8. My trip to Italy helped improve my self-confidence. I learned that I could rely on myself and that I could deal with new and unusual situations. I came back a stronger person than I was before.

9. It has been absolutely necessary for me to make some changes in my lifestyle in order to find personal satisfaction. For years, I had put off things I most wanted to do. Finally, I had to change this state of affairs.

10. At noon, I found myself sitting under the broken sundial, drinking coffee from a paper cup. Clouds came drifting in warm and low; crows continually called out, hidden among the feathery, light-bearing branches of the spring trees. This is always the time of year when the world suddenly shows me spring, and I see it particularly in these branches engraved against the pale sky. After a whole winter, I look at them very closely: they have compelled me to look.

List the questions that still need to be answered for the inadequately developed paragraphs of Exercise 2.

Example: Inadequate paragraph: My grandmother was a remarkable woman. She embodied the best of the pioneer spirit and left a legacy of independence for her children and grandchildren.

Questions: What is the "best of the pioneer spirit"? What specific action or actions show this spirit in the grandmother? What is the "legacy of independence"?

Using one or more of the previously discussed methods of developing paragraphs, rewrite one of the inadequately developed paragraphs from Exercise 2. Make sure that your paragraph expresses a complete and understandable idea and that it answers the questions listed in Exercise 3.

NAME _____ DATE _____

Rearrange the following confused essay into unified, coherent, adequately developed paragraphs. You may change sentence order, provide necessary connections and transitions, and omit any irrelevant material. Mark the topic sentence of each of your revised paragraphs with an asterisk.

Beowulf lived in a world that was ruled by a strong sense of mortality. Those who became heroes were blessed with superior strength, discernment, and foresight. Death was a powerful influence on their world view. Life was rough, and death was most often violent. Every man in this culture was a warrior, and often young men achieved their status and property through their prowess in war. To be a coward was one of the worst sins that a man could commit. Their attitude was not one of total despair: they had a very firm feeling that order was possible in spite of human conflicts and destructive natural phenomena. The climate they lived in was harsh—the winters were both long and cold; the people lived in wooden buildings warmed by open fires. These people realized that they had "forethought" and "discernment" to help them survive. These qualities form the basis for the personal courage, the social justice and the personal relationships these people developed. In *Beowulf* these qualities are often expressed through the use of light and dark imagery and the characters' speeches on wisdom and the right way to live. Beowulf's society can be compared to that of early Germanic tribes and pre-Islamic Arabic tribes. In *Beowulf* the lord-thane relationship stabilizes society. The lord had to demonstrate physical prowess, courage, and generosity. The retainers served their lord loyally to the death and counselled him at need. When one considers the everyday life of Beowulf and his companions, the first impression might be that eating, drinking, sleeping, sailing, and fighting were the only things they thought about. This poem does show aspects of the life of this society that were most important to its members and that they wished to preserve for future generations. Deeds were always performed for the sake of the social group and a strong sense of community always existed among the people of a tribe. The strong who kept their loyalty intact and lived and fought together were the only ones who could hope to conquer the forces that threatened them with extinction.

Your rewritten essay:

Punctuation

USE OF THE COMMA

---

1 Use of the comma with coordinate or correlative conjunctions

---

When independent clauses are joined by a coordinate conjunction (**and, but, for, or, nor, yet, so**) or by correlative conjunctions (**either . . . or, neither . . . nor, not only . . . but**), a comma is placed before the conjunction.

Susan felt isolated for about a week, but later she began to like living so far from town.

I'm going to Bentonville tonight, so I may be late getting home.

If pairs of words, phrases, or dependent clauses are joined by only a correlative conjunction or a coordinating conjunction, there should be **no comma before the conjunction. Notice that there is no comma before the conjunctions that join the following pairs.**

I grew **peppers** and **tomatoes** in the garden last year. (*words*)

Anyone **who wants to canoe** but **who doesn't know how to swim** must wear a life jacket. (*dependent clauses*)

My book is either **under the bed** or **behind the bookcase**. (*prepositional phrases*)

His **dog** and **cat play** and **eat** together. (*words*)

If the independent clauses are very short, the comma may be eliminated. For example:

They stayed but I went.

---

2 Use of the comma after introductory sentence elements

Use a comma after an introductory phrase, word, or subordinate clause. This comma makes the sentence easier to read and may prevent misunderstanding the sentence. The comma often clarifies the meaning of a sentence. For example:

> Beyond the ocean stretched to the distant horizon.

Rewrite:
> Beyond, the ocean stretched to the distant horizon.

Without a comma following **beyond**, it would be easy to assume that this sentence begins with a prepositional phrase, **beyond the ocean.** This reading, of course, does not make sense. We can prevent that misreading by putting a comma after the introductory word.

---

3 Use of the comma in a series

Use a comma between words, phrases, or clauses that appear in a series of three or more coordinate items.

a. Finally, we realized that George had already gone, that he had taken the car, and that we would have to walk home.
(*a series of three noun clauses*)

b. The box contained four old hats, a number of newspapers, eight buttons, and a green umbrella.
(*a series of four noun phrases*)

c. The red, yellow, pink, and fuchsia roses won prizes.
(*a series of four coordinate adjectives*)

Notice that a slight difference in meaning in the following two sentences is indicated by the position of the final comma in the series.

For the picnic, they cooked potato salad, fried chicken, ham, and eggs.

For the picnic, they cooked potato salad, fried chicken, ham and eggs.

Commas are also used between and after the numbers of a date.

We entered the city on August 3, 1848, at 11:00 in the morning.

---

4 Use of the comma with restrictive and nonrestrictive modifiers

---

A nonrestrictive clause, phrase, or appositive gives additional information about the noun it modifies, but that information is not needed to identify the person, place, or thing designated by the noun. A restrictive clause, phrase, or appositive **does** supply information essential for identifying the person, place, or thing designated by the noun that it modifies. Notice the difference in meaning in these two sentences.

My sister who is an airline pilot left for India yesterday.
(The writer here has more than one sister, and the relative clause is needed to identify which one is being discussed.)

Rewrite:
My sister, who is an airline pilot, left for India yesterday.
(In this case, there is only one sister; the relative clause gives extra information about her, but this information is not necessary to identify her.)

Nonrestrictive adjective clauses, phrases, and appositives are set off by commas; restrictive adjective modifiers are not. For example:

Mary, my best friend, has left town for three days.
(In this sentence, the appositive phrase **my best friend** supplies some additional but dispensable information about Mary. Mary is identified by her name.)

Rewrite:
My friend Mary has left town for three days.
(In this sentence, the name **Mary** is needed to identify which friend is being talked about.)

5 Use of commas with parenthetical and interrupting elements

Often a word or phrase or clause will interrupt the rhythm of a sentence. There is no hard and fast rule about use of commas in these situations, so you must use your own judgment. You must decide whether or not the tone and emphasis you are trying to achieve warrant the use of commas.

The high cost of housing, **generally speaking,** prohibits middle income families from purchasing new homes.

Brenda's new job, **if I may say so,** is taking too much time.

Well, he did say he'd come.

The new saplings, **of course,** will die in this heat.

NAME _____ DATE _____

Supply all necessary commas in the following sentences. If a sentence is written correctly, place a *C* beside it in the margin.

1. We got to the cabin quickly for the roads had been cleared of snow.

2. John is a good student but he's too lazy to work hard at anything he dislikes.

3. Where he went that summer and what he did there are things no one ever found out.

4. Class is over and we are ready to go home.

5. The cat won't come out of the tree nor can anyone climb up after it.

6. Come out at once or I'll huff and I'll puff and I'll blow your house down.

7. I particularly like days when the sun is bright and reflects from the lake.

8. My grandparents' farm burned in 1893 yet the chimney is still standing to mark the homestead.

9. The top of the mountain is a long way from here and we've walked fifteen miles so I think we should wait until tomorrow to go up.

10. I thought he said to close the door so I did.

11. She had passed the old house many times but had never seen anyone there.

12. I'd like to leave town early tomorrow so I'll have to set my alarm for 5:00 A.M.

13. Everyone stopped working when the storm began and the lights went out.

14. John and Mary wanted to leave Friday morning but Susan and Jim said they'd rather wait until Monday or not go at all.

15. This is a fine day to go huckleberrying but tomorrow will be even better.

Compose ten sentences of your own: five showing use of the comma with a coordinate conjunction and five showing coordination of elements within the sentence that do not require the use of the comma.

1.

2.

3.

4.

5.

6.

7.

8.

9.

10.

Supply commas where they are needed in the following sentences.

1. Inside the fire was burning brightly.

2. Seeing a moose for the first time he recognized it immediately.

3. However you may feel about it the highway will be built next to your property.

4. While eating my dogs are oblivious to the people around them.

5. Before you can open your presents you must blow out the candles on the cake.

6. Actually today is not a holiday but I think I'll go fishing anyway.

7. Riding over the hill the cavalry saw the fort beside the river.

8. To be honest I don't know.

9. When he comes in jump out and shout, "Surprise!"

10. Before reading the magazines everyone wants to get comfortable.

11. Before anyone could stop him he had leaped into the river.

12. When angry or frustrated cats lash their tails.

13. By the time the moon rose over the mountain everyone was asleep.

14. Of the twenty new recruits fifteen had gone to college.

15. After the visit to the doctor the baby's health improved.

Compose five sentences of your own showing the use of the comma after introductory words, phrases, or subordinate clauses.

1.

2.

3.

4.

5.

Supply the necessary commas in the following sentences.

1. A newspaper dated November 14 1972 was lying on the floor.

2. The giraffe has a short body long legs and an elongated neck.

3. Her sewing basket overflowed with thread buttons needles pins and hooks and eyes.

4. It's obvious that no one is at home that the doors are locked and that we will have to wait on the front porch.

5. She said she had to cook dinner clean the living room dining room and bathroom and put the children to bed.

6. The articles I wanted were in *Harper's* April 18 1963 and *Life* June 4 1972.

7. The teacher gave 2 A's 8 B's 7 C's and 3 D's.

8. Cats dogs mice and hedgehogs may all be domesticated.

9. Shoes ships sealing wax cabbages and kings were what the walrus talked about.

10. Apples pears oranges filberts and walnuts are all in the salad.

11. The new magazine titles *Outdoors The Northwest* and *Fishing* were catalogued immediately.

12. All the couples arrived safely: Marsha and Bob Joyce and Fred Barbara and George.

13. Marie reminisced over her high school prom picture the gold and blue pom pons the old class ring and David's football picture.

14. To date the shipments arrived on the third sixth and eighth of April and on the ninth eleventh and twelfth of May.

15. Ninety percent of all nursing pharmacy and x-ray technology students passed their exams.

Compose five sentences of your own that illustrate the use of the comma in a series.

1.

2.

3.

4.

5.

Supply necessary commas or delete unnecessary commas in the following sentences. If a sentence is written correctly, put a *C* beside it in the margin.

1. Just before lighting the candles, she turned to her sister who smiled and said, "Go ahead."

2. The beefalo a cross between cattle and buffalo is an experimental animal.

3. The name Grimalkin is usually reserved for cats.

4. People who have no children are often the most outspoken in discussing child-rearing with people, who are parents.

5. Clothes which are out of style just clutter up a closet.

6. My father who is a painter is a very talented man.

7. Nancy my only cousin is an electrician.

8. These tennis shoes old and worn as they are are still the most comfortable shoes I have.

9. He chose the piece of cake that Ellen wanted.

10. My brother wanted to take his vacation in San Francisco his favorite city.

11. The dinner party which had been planned for weeks went smoothly.

12. In order to accommodate the new guests who just arrived the clerk opened a new wing of rooms.

13. The books, mentioned in the review, were available at Bob's Book Store.

14. The clerk who always helps me chose the lilac dress for my debut at the opera.

15. My friend, Joshua, fell and broke his leg.

NAME _____ DATE _____

Compose five sentences of your own showing the use of nonrestrictive modifiers; then compose five showing the use of restrictive modifiers.

1.

2.

3.

4.

5.

6.

7.

8.

9.

10.

Punctuation

USE OF THE SEMICOLON

The main use of the semicolon is to link two independent clauses (those clauses which have complete thoughts and both subjects and verbs) that are related in idea and are not joined by a coordinating conjunction.

John sold me his old skiis last spring, he's moving to Florida in September.

Rewrite:
John sold me his old skiis last spring; he's moving to Florida in September.

Only **independent** clauses are so linked.

I like to sing while I wash dishes.

(No semicolon is needed here because the second clause, **while I wash dishes**, is a dependent clause.)

A semicolon can also be used when the second independent clause is introduced by a connective word or phrase such as **hence, therefore, moreover, then, on the other hand, however, for example, nevertheless, in fact**. Sometimes, as in the following examples, a comma is put **after** the connecting word.

I've been to New York many times, however, I've never spent a night there.

Rewrite:
I've been to New York many times; however, I've never spent a night there.

It began to grow dark and stormy nevertheless the Boy Scouts kept on walking.

Rewrite:
It began to grow dark and stormy; nevertheless, the Boy Scouts kept on walking.

Supply the necessary punctuation in the following sentences.

1. A loud crackle came over the loudspeaker it was followed by a confused noise of laughing and singing.

2. Painting is more than just a hobby for her she intends to go to art school and become a professional artist.

3. He should be here any minute in fact here he is now.

4. There are some curious animals in Australia for example the wombat.

5. There are some curious animals in out-of-the-way places for example the wombat lives in Australia.

6. There was not a light in the house a curious clanking sound came from the staircase outside the storm continued to rage.

7. Five people came to the meeting then someone asked, "Do we have a quorum?"

8. I went walking in the fields yesterday on the way back I saw a fox.

9. He left the house in such a hurry that he forgot his key luckily he had hidden an extra one in the garage.

10. Where have you been how long did you stay and what will you do now?

11. She left for the Orient however she never arrived.

12. Flannery O'Connor's short stories are superb she is a master of the character sketch.

13. The school bus drivers were striking for better working conditions they wanted the students to be more polite and quieter.

14. Mr. Brown submitted the necessary credentials moreover he sent out extra letters of reference.

15. The city residents were dissatisfied with the county's new tax increase they wanted to keep taxes at a minimum.

Compose ten sentences of your own: five that illustrate the use of the semicolon to link independent clauses that are not joined by a coordinating conjunction and five that illustrate the use of the semicolon with conjunctive adverbs (like *however*, *therefore*, and so on).

1.

2.

3.

4.

5.

6.

7.

8.

9.

10.

In the following paragraphs there are five errors in the use of the semicolon. Circle the errors and rewrite the sentences correctly in the space provided below.

On the first evening we spent by the lake, three sandhill cranes flew over our campsite, their cries have a wild, prehistoric sound. Earlier in the day, we had seen their tracks, hieroglyphic and precise, in the mud pools along the road. After the cranes had passed, the sky darkened. Lightning flashed off to the north; but no rain fell close to us. We had the stars instead and a late quarter moon. All night long it moved slowly up behind the pines, and at dawn it stood above the trees; the sun to the east, the moon to the west.

Sunrise was a struggle. Should I stay awake and watch the sun come up or root, pig-like, back into my sleeping bag? Aesthetics won, generally speaking. My reward was the return flight of an owl, I couldn't see what kind. He'd caught something; his feet hung low, clutching his prey; his wings working strongly and noiselessly.

Punctuation

USE OF THE COLON

The colon is normally used to enumerate, explain, illustrate, or extend an idea that has already been mentioned. The main clause of the sentence will appear before the colon and will often contain a word signaling the use of the colon, such as **several**, **some**, **one**, **these**, **the following**, and so on. A grammatically complete sentence must precede the colon. The colon can substitute for the word **namely** and **that is**. Note the following examples:

Their goal was clear: they intended to cross the river before nightfall.

Here the colon acts as a coordinator linking two independent clauses into a compound sentence.

We wanted to leave the city for several reasons: it was noisy, the cost of living was high, and the crime rate was rising.

Here the colon signals a list to follow.

Do not use a colon after a linking verb or a preposition.

Some of the most popular animals for pets are: dogs, cats, hamsters, and turtles.

Rewrite:
The following are some of the most popular animals for pets: dogs, cats, hamsters, and turtles.

Some of the most popular animals for pets are dogs, cats, hamsters, and turtles.

Yesterday my aunt told me about: going to the opera in Milan and visiting the cathedral there.

Rewrite:
Yesterday my aunt told me about two experiences: going to the opera in Milan and visiting the cathedral there.

or

Yesterday my aunt told me about going to the opera in Milan and visiting the cathedral there.

NAME _____ DATE _____

Supply or delete colons where necessary in the following sentences, correcting any faulty punctuation.

1. Only one person met me at the airport my brother.

2. Some herbs commonly used in salads are: basil, savory, parsley, and dill.

3. She told me her lifelong ambition to be an astronaut.

4. The school board said that next year the metropolitan schools will concentrate on basics: that is, reading, writing, and arithmetic.

5. The tour group will be visiting these cities in Italy, Rome, Venice, Florence, Padua, and Naples.

6. There are only two things I fear bears and rattlesnakes.

7. Several authors appeared at the opening Smith, Jones, and Taylor.

8. The shoppers demanded refunds for the faulty products that is, they wanted their money's worth or their money refunded.

9. All the family members gathered for Thanksgiving dinner Grandma and Grandpa, Mom and Dad, Susie, Frank, and Rex.

10. The following figures represent the latest poll—55% for Brown, 42% for Doe, and 3% undecided.

Rewrite or combine the following sentences so that each contains a correctly used colon. You may have to change the wording of the sentence to allow the introduction of a colon.

Example: My favorite colors are green and yellow.
            I have two favorite colors: green and yellow.

1. He gave us explicit directions to the museum. He told us to go three blocks north, turn right, and walk five blocks, then to turn left at a big red brick building.

2. Mary said three things made yesterday evening a lovely one. She ate dinner out, went dancing, and drove around the lake by moonlight.

3. The only thing you can do with a broken ski pole is throw it away.

4. Mark especially likes to read about pirates and about famous sea battles.

5. Our vacation plans include four days on the Washington coast, a ferry ride to Vancouver, and a drive through British Columbia.

NAME _____ DATE _____

Compose ten sentences of your own showing correct use of the colon. Include three sentences that list items and three compound sentences.

1.

2.

3.

4.

5.

6.

7.

8.

9.

10.

Punctuation

USE OF THE DASH

The dash is used primarily to mark sudden or emphatic pauses or breaks in a sentence. It may show:

A. A break or reversal in the line of thought,

The wagon came careening over the hill toward the station—but too late, for the train was just pulling out of sight.

B. A more dramatic interruption in the sentence flow than the use of commas indicates,

The first settlers, according to the most reliable accounts, arrived in 1856.

Rewrite:
The first settlers—all the most reliable accounts give this date—arrived in 1856.

C. A summary or amplification of the preceding statement.

Gentians, spring beauties, trillium, camass—all these early flowers—are the first tokens of spring.

The unusual house—the sugar-laced windows, the gingerbread walls, the neatly iced front door—lured the children closer and closer.

Because dashes are used to mark emphasis, they should be used cautiously. Too many dashes will lessen the effect of emphasis. When typing text, make a dash by using two hyphens (hyphen -; dash - -) with no space before, between, or after the hyphens.

NAME _____ DATE _____

Supply the appropriate punctuation for the following sentences.

1. Growing squash no matter what anyone says to the contrary is extremely easy.

2. Too many people these days I firmly believe this refuse to read.

3. Rare sea shells, oriental fans, pieces of raw silk, coral all the treasures of the East fill the old chest.

4. Anyone who wants to succeed in this class and I hope everyone does should attend regularly.

5. She filled her living room with knick-knacks and French Provincial furniture not my style at all.

6. The New York subway murders most people will remember the newspaper headlines were never solved.

7. Of the 10,000 citizens who are all registered voters only 45% voted in last week's election.

8. Lora called together her parents, aunts and uncles, brothers and sisters all of her family to announce her wedding plans.

9. The trip had been dreary and dismal but suddenly the sun brought brightness and gaiety.

10. Nearly all the zoo animals wily cats, clever monkeys, thunderous elephants fell prey to the epidemic.

NAME _____ DATE _____

Using dashes, insert the material in parentheses in the preceding sentences.

Example: One hundred and forty people were invited to the meeting. (Only forty came.)

One hundred and forty people were invited to the meeting—only forty came.

1. Everyone who comes to the Homecoming game will receive a pennant in the school colors. (We expect several hundred people, at least.)

2. John said that Cecil was sure to win a scholarship. (I'm sure he's right.)

3. You were very kind to me when I was sad and lonely. (More kind than I deserved.)

4. June, July, and August are my favorite months. (The bright, hot midsummer months.)

5. He loaned me his car yesterday. (A big, lumbering, red monster.)

6. The lights went out suddenly and we were left to fend on our own. (Just as the wizard predicted.)

7. This year's garden was a great success. (Juicy tomatoes, tender peas, tasty beans, succulent squash.)

8. Twenty-three of the new members had not paid their annual dues. (A pattern not to be tolerated.)

9. The state of Wyoming is full of contradictions. (Bustling highways and quiet rivers, condominiums and log cabins.)

10. The new offices, new staff, new publicity was causing an uproar among the old-timers. (The whole new state of affairs.)

Compose ten sentences of your own that illustrate the correct use of the dash.

1.

2.

3.

4.

5.

6.

7.

8.

9.

10.

In the following paragraphs, place the appropriate punctuation marks in the proper places.

A. There was one year when spring missed us altogether. The dull dreary foggy mornings felt particularly lonely the kind of loneliness that gnaws at one's soul. The rains left the countryside drenched in a sweet vapor however the coldness dampened that potential pleasantness. All of the spring plants sprouted slowly snow bells crocus daffodils. But either the fog obscured their message of spring or the coldness delayed the oncoming of spring. In either case we found it hard to feel the lighthearted friendliness of previous springs. Nothing remarkable stood out about that spring no rainbows no caterpillars not even a spring robin. Then suddenly it was summer one day it was gray and dull and the next it was bright and sultry. Spring was skipped over in favor of the hot summer. Finally in June when everyone realized spring must be past we too saw that there would be no delightful days of anticipation and yearning the real spring feelings.

B. Commencement was of course the most exciting day for the graduating seniors. During the past four years the long study hours grueling tests and long term papers seemed never-ending. There were times when each senior thought of quitting or changing majors or just not caring any more. It seemed to them that this graduation day would never arrive. But now as their names were called and they marched across the stage the hard work of the past four years was diminished by new challenges. Most of these seniors were looking forward to jobs or graduate school. Some would be taking jobs in their own hometowns some would be moving to large metropolitan areas some would be going overseas. They all would be engaged in new challenging experiences.

C. Of the fifty-five entries only three were chosen as finalists they would each receive $10,000. These finalists were now ready for the grand prize drawing. The studio was packed to the brim the final entrants were on stage and the emcee was ready. The three huge boxes decorated in gaudy flags flowers and sparklers were lined up in front of the contestants. By choosing one of these boxes the correct one someone would win the big prize $100,000 yearly for the rest of her or his life. The emcee read the rules for the fourth time. The tension mounted. Melba from Arkansas chose Box #1 so did Frank from Connecticut and Steve from New Mexico opted for Box #3. Now they each waited rather breathlessly as the emcee removed the boxes. Melba and Fred had won baby elephants Steve won a trip to Cleveland. None had chosen the grand prize in Box #2. Disappointed they all filed off the stage and were sadly greeted by their families and friends.

Mechanics

ITEMS 80, 81, 82, and 84

QUOTATION MARKS

---

1 **The period or comma always goes inside the closing quotation mark.**

Direct discourse (actual speech or conversation) is enclosed in quotation marks. Indirect discourse does not need quotation marks because you are being told only the gist of a conversation, not the actual speech.

Direct: Professor Taylor said, "The test scores were high."

Indirect: Professor Taylor told his students that the test scores were high.

The rule for commas and periods is followed no matter what grammatical structure is being enclosed within quotation marks. Whether the quotation marks enclose a complete sentence or only one word, the period or comma is placed inside the last quotation mark. For example:

   "I know", she said, "that you are telling me a barefaced lie".

Rewrite:
   "I know," she said, "that you are telling me a barefaced lie."

   He was a "bluebeard", vicious and calculating in his cruelty.

Rewrite:
   He was a "bluebeard," vicious and calculating in his cruelty.

In the case of a quotation within a quotation, both the single and double quotation marks are placed outside the comma or period. See the examples below:

> The professor said, "I recently read that Samuel Johnson said of Shakespeare's plays, 'Shakespeare has united the powers of exciting laughter and sorrow not only in one mind, but in one composition'."

Rewrite:
> The professor said, "I recently read that Samuel Johnson said of Shakespeare's plays, 'Shakespeare has united the powers of exciting laughter and sorrow not only in one mind, but in one composition.' "

---

2 The colon or semicolon always goes outside the closing quotation mark.

As you will notice, this convention is just the opposite of use for the comma or period. Note the following examples:

> He called the schedule of activities his "load:" work, study, exercise, recreation, and sleep.

Rewrite:
> He called the schedule of activities his "load": work, study, exercise, recreation, and sleep.

---

3 The question mark sometimes goes inside, sometimes outside, the closing quotation mark.

Therefore, you must decide individually each case where a question mark and quotation marks are used. The following conventions will help explain the criteria for deciding where to place the question mark:

a. Who was it that said, "I regret that I have but one life to lose for my country"?
(When the whole sentence, but not the quotation, is a question, the question mark is placed **outside** the closing quotation mark.)

b. He asked her bluntly, "Will you marry me?"
(When the unit within the quotation marks is a question, the question mark goes **inside** the closing quotation mark. Also note that there is no additional punctuation following the quotation mark. INCORRECT: He asked her bluntly, "Will you marry me?".)

c. When will they stop asking, "Who then is responsible for the war?" (When both the whole sentence and the unit enclosed in quotation marks are questions, **one** question mark is placed **inside** the closing quotation mark. And again there is no additional punctuation following the final quotation mark.)

---

4 The titles of articles, short stories, short poems, songs, chapters of books, and episodes of radio and television programs should be enclosed in quotation marks.

You should not, however, enclose the title of a paper handed into a class instructor in quotation marks except if the title is a direct quotation. If a title of an article, for example, appears to need additional surrounding punctuation (i.e., period, comma, colon, semicolon), the same above rules apply. Note the following examples:

a. Thomas Gray's "Elegy Written in a Country Churchyard" is reputed to be the most anthologized poem in the English language.

b. *Process and Thought in Composition,* Chapter 1, "Invention: Preliminary Considerations," describes how to select a paper topic to students.

c. So many jazz musicians have improvised the famous song, "Georgia on My Mind."

NAME _____ DATE _____

In the following sentences place commas, periods, colons, semicolons, question marks, and quotation marks in their proper places. If necessary, capitalize words. Reading the sentence out loud may help you in placing the punctuation marks.

1. Mary screamed over and over I don't believe you

2. Everyone was asking how long can this fiasco go on

3. Marvin searched the *Reader's Guide to Periodical Literature* and found an article entitled Solar Energy The Plan for the Future which would be helpful

4. The plane Bill observed did not have the proper equipment

5. Eighty-three of the one hundred participants said the lawn mower started nine out of ten times

6. Steven always called his mother Momsie

7. If we were to purchase this acreage asked Fred how long would it take for the land to increase its value

8. As the French teacher lectured on Baudelaire he said Baudelaire's influence on the French Symbolist movement is discussed in Jones' essay Baudelaire and the Symbolists

9. I hate her yelled Emma

10. I don't like her either replied John but it's your life

NAME _____ DATE _____

In the following sentences place commas, periods, colons, semicolons, question marks, and quotation marks in their proper places. If necessary, capitalize words. Reading the sentence out loud may help you in placing the punctuation marks.

1. The doctor who was lecturing said place the scalpel slightly to the left of the incision

2. Chapter 3 was entitled Men and Women

3. Orwell's *1984* is a book said Mr. James that is uncanny in its representation of modern politics

4. In discussing his gardening technique Charles said what you basically need is good soil don't you think

5. Ralph asked again aren't you angry with me

6. He yelled back to his companions I can do it however he slipped and broke his leg

7. The used-car salesman was clever in saying you won't find a car in better shape that is this old shall we write it up for you

8. The resort town was filled with ladies laden with make-up who said when is the sun going to shine

9. Can this be all she asked

10. The sociologist said the *c'est la vie* attitude of most modern men results in their saying So what

In the following paragraphs place commas, periods, question marks, and quotation marks in their proper places.

Every summer the Summer Repertory Theatre hired a guest director to help with the production; this year the famous (or infamous) George Lamont was invited to conduct Shakespeare's *King Lear* Mr. Lamont was having some difficulty in working with the meager lot of amateur performers The first problem developed with Act I, scene 1

Mr. Lamont said to Betsy playing the part of Goneril My dear you must emphasize the shallowness *and* cleverness of Goneril's speech Don't just say Sir, I love you more than words can wield the matter Emphasize the key words: love words wield matter

Oh Betsy insisted I am interpreting Goneril's character as a woman who is rather nonchalant dull if you will Don't you feel that's appropriate

Enraged Lamont rushed toward Betsy screaming What do you think you're doing Goneril Nonchalant Bah Can such a nonchalant woman conceive a plot to blind a poor old man

Betsy was somewhat put off by Mr. Lamont's insistence that she read exactly as he demanded She asked How is this play being directed Aren't the actors' interpretations valuable guidelines for the director

Your indignance my young woman huffed Lamont is beyond my comprehension Shall we try the lines this way Emphasize all the *the's* in your speech

Mechanics

ITALICS

A special type, italic (slanted letters), is used to set off certain words in a sentence from other words that are printed in regular roman type (upright letters). In handwriting or typewriting, italicized words are indicated by underlining them. Note the following instances in which words should be italicized (that is, underlined).

---

1 **The titles of books, newspapers, magazines, professional journals, plays, long poems, movies, radio programs, television programs, long musical compositions (usually classical), works of art, and ships should be italicized by underlining.**

For example,
a. The weekly magazines *Time* and *Newsweek* are comparable. (magazines)

b. The lecture discussed the nature imagery in William Wordsworth's *The Prelude*. (long poem)

c. Dvorak's *New World Symphony,* conducted by the young maestro, brought superlative reviews in the *New York Times*. (musical composition, newspaper)

d. Ibsen's famous play *Hedda Gabler* was scheduled to play April 21–30 in Boston. (play)

e. Rodin's *Balzac* rests in the Museum of Modern Art in New York City. (sculpture)

2   Also italicize words referred to as words.

This convention is used to distinguish a word being discussed from a word serving a special function in a sentence. Note the different meanings in the following sentences:

He questioned the appropriateness of honesty in this context.

(The question is whether or not a certain behavior, honesty, is appropriate for a particular situation.)

He questioned the appropriateness of *honesty* in this context.

(The question is whether or not the word *honesty* is appropriate.)

As you can see, you must be careful in distinguishing a particular word when you are discussing it.

3   Italicize foreign words and phrases, unless they have become naturalized or Anglicized.

This convention is followed so that a reader may not be confused or startled by the sudden entry of a strange-looking word. However, some foreign words have become part of the English language through their extensive use. These words do not have to be italicized: habeas corpus, mania, siesta, subpoena. Most dictionaries will indicate which foreign words and phrases have become naturalized. Obviously, then, you should check a dictionary if you're unsure of a foreign word.

NAME _____ DATE _____

Those words or phrases that need italics should be underlined. If necessary, check the information in a dictionary.

1. The advertising agents could not decide whether to place their advertisement in McCall's, House and Garden, or Gourmet.

2. Although the William Tell Overture is a famous musical piece, it is not often played for concerts.

3. The bibliography indicated that more specific information could be found in Studies in Romanticism.

4. The Art Institute of Chicago owns American Gothic, a painting by Grant Wood, and On the Terrace by Renoir.

5. Fibber McGee and Molly is an old, yet important radio program.

6. The linguist carefully studied the relationship between thee and thou.

7. Marian's attitude toward a life with ten adopted children was c'est la vie.

8. The concept of detente is unclear to many Americans.

9. The instructor deducted points for misspellings of there, their, and they're.

10. "Bon vivant," screamed the crippled old lady, as she was carried away in the taxi.

11. "Ain't Love Grand" is a M*A*S*H episode highlighting Klinger and Major Winchester.

12. Julia Child always ends her television program by saying "Bon Appetit."

13. Its and it's are often confused with each other.

14. E.T. has been nationally acclaimed for its ingenious portrait of an alien.

15. The President's wife was selected to christen the new yacht Gloria.

NAME _____ DATE _____

Those words or phrases that need italics should be underlined. If necessary, check the information in a dictionary.

1. Bill considered his new-found interest in ballet his raison d'etre.

2. The New York Times was first in presenting a comprehensive view of the blackout.

3. There was an unusually strong esprit de corps among the young recruits.

4. The Washington Post continued to misspell tangent as target.

5. Frank presented his paper, "Nature Imagery in Shakespeare's The Tempest," for the third time.

6. The old English teacher was determined to have her students distinguish between its and it's.

7. If a Frenchman were to see Marge for the first time, he would exclaim "Quelle jeune fille!"

8. The New York Times glowingly reviewed the opening of Ibsen's famous play Hedda Gabler.

9. The Sturm and Drang movement in German literature produced the classic melodramatic novel, The Sorrows of Werther.

10. Diane found the Guide to English Literature helpful when she compiled a bibliography on D. H. Lawrence in Italy.

Proofread the following paragraphs, underlining those words and phrases that should be italicized.

Professor Foster taught English 203: The Research Paper in such a manner that students never knew they were working with difficult material. First, he spent time in the library's reference section familiarizing students with the Encyclopedia Britannica and the Encyclopedia Americana. One particularly useful research tool is the Library of Congress Subject Headings which will give related topics where one might find additional information. Other general references include bibliographies, dictionaries, and biographies.

As David researched his topic on Chaucer in the card catalog, he found A Reading of the Canterbury Tales by Bernard Huppe and Donaldson's book Chaucer's Poetry. Since the paper was to focus on the language in Chaucer's Canterbury Tales, such word forms as complexion, meaning one's temperament, and humour, meaning one's state of health, were of particular interest to David's research. He discovered the Oxford English Dictionary in the reference section to be a useful source in beginning his research.

Mechanics

HYPHENS

Hyphens are distinguished from dashes in that they are shorter and they function differently. Hyphens are used (1) to mark compound words, and (2) to divide words at the end of lines.

---

1 There are different types of compound words. Note the examples of the following compound words:

A. Two or more words functioning as a single grammatical unit.
  1. The **two-year-old** spilled her orange juice. (noun)
  2. Even the **blue-ribbon** jury had a difficult decision. (adjective)
  3. The commander **second-guessed** his opponent's tactics. (verb)
  4. The principal made the decision **open-mindedly.** (adverb)

B. Two-word numbers (from 21–99) when they are written out.
thirty-two, fifty-five, eighty-six

C. Combinations with prefixes **ex-** and **self-**.
ex-convict, **ex-**president, **self-**effacing, **self-**concern

D. Combinations with prefixes like **anti-**, **pro-**, **pre-**, **post-**, when the second element begins with a capital letter or number.
anti-Establishment, **pro-**French, **pre-**1865, **post-**1955

E. Combinations with prefixes like **anti-**, **pro-**, **pre-**, **re-**, **semi-**, when the second element begins with the letter that occurs at the end of the prefix.

anti-intellectual, **semi-**independent, **re-**entry

F. Combinations where unhyphenated compound words might be mistaken for another word.
   1. I'd like to **re-cover** the old chair.
      I wish I could **recover** my lost purse.
   2. The contract must be **re-signed** immediately to be valid.
      The president **resigned** his position.

---

2   Syllabification

Hyphens also divide words at the end of lines, but only at a syllable break. One-syllable words can never be broken and hyphenated and a word should not be broken if only one or two letters remain on a line. The dictionary indicates how many syllables a word has and where the divisions occur. Always check your dictionary when you are unsure of word divisions. There are several helpful hints about word divisions:

A. After prefixes (pre-, im-, in-, post-)

pre-na-tal, post-pone, pre-scrip-tion, im-pend

B. Before a suffix (-tion, -ment, -less, -ing)

men-tion, mon-u-ment, pre-par-ing

C. Between double consonants

oc-cur-rence, cop-per, pro-fes-sor

NAME _____ DATE _____

Place hyphens where necessary to clarify the meaning and eliminate ambiguity.

1. The easy to read books were placed on the second floor.

2. Harold always bought wash and wear suits.

3. The secretary made certain an up to date report was prepared for the meetings on the twenty fifth of each month.

4. The six to eight week cruise began on May 31.

5. The pre Columbian art exhibit was on a New York to San Francisco tour.

6. Mr. Franklin was an exteacher from Pennsylvania roaming about in his ready made van.

7. The Smith sisters were seventy two on August 24.

8. The self examination took two hours and was followed by another selftest.

9. Reentry into the apartment was very difficult.

10. The antiintellectual movement failed miserably in the pre 1955 era.

11. The exnun was now teaching in the Minneapolis St. Paul area.

12. The child's grandmother told her the newly seeded flower bed was a no no.

13. The half hour conference ended with each committee member resigning the new contract.

14. He was a good for nothing loser and a lowdown scoundrel.

15. The lowcost housing enabled fifty two poor families to live more comfortably.

Check the syllabification of the following words in your dictionary. How many of these words may be divided at the end of a line? How may they be divided?

advocate   nebulous

boa   orient

calliope   pall-mall

decorative   quandary

electrolysis   rappel

fortuitous   safe

gene   teen-ager

handy   unanimous

incipient   various

jeopardy   wall-eyed

kosher   Xray

lip-read   yeoman

martyr   zodiac

In the following paragraph there are errors in hyphenation. Find the errors and correct them.

Stan is a man who is easily persuaded by up to date issues. Since the preVietnam War days, Stan has tried to reorder his lifestyle around would be radical organizations. He was antiEstablishment and proDemocracy; he was antiMao and proNixon and proMcGovern; he was semireformed and overrefined. In every case, Stan only wanted a temporary label so his life would be ready made, ready to order, clear cut. However, in recent years he has begun a self examination program in which he open mindedly reentered his previous so called stances through an extrasensory, time projection technique. Who knows what his next position will be, but perhaps someday Stan will find his island in the sun.

Mechanics

NUMBERS

There are certain conventions regarding the use of numbers in written copy, and they should be followed consistently. Notice the rules for putting numbers in written copy.

1 **Spell out a number at the beginning of a sentence; do not use an Arabic numeral.**

824 women attended the convention for NOW.

Rewrite:
Eight hundred and twenty-four women attended the convention for NOW.

2 **Spell out any number if less than three digits (less than 101) when the number is used as an adjective modifying a noun.**

During the first half of the **20th** century, **28 4**-year colleges and **14 2**-year colleges adopted collective bargaining.

Rewrite:
During the first half of the **twentieth** century **twenty-eight four**-year colleges and **fourteen two**-year colleges adopted collective bargaining.

3   **Always use Arabic numerals with** A.M. **(or a.m.) and** P.M. **(or p.m.) and do not add the redundant** *o'clock* **and** *morning* **and** *afternoon.*

John's first class began at **ten** A.M. in the morning.

Rewrite:
John's first class began at **10:00** A.M.

4   **Use Arabic numerals for dates and page numbers.**

The date, July **fourth, seventeen hundred and seventy-six**, appears frequently on pages **thirty-two, forty-eight**, and **ninety-one** of the history text.

Rewrite:
The date July **4, 1776**, appears frequently on pages **32, 48**, and **91** of the history text.

5   **Use Arabic numerals for addresses, dollars and cents, decimals, degrees, measurements, and percentages.**

Janice lives at **2587** Pine Street. (address)

Tom paid **$11.75** for his new taillight. (dollars and cents)

The Dow-Jones went up **2.14** this morning. (decimals)

As you drive down the dirt road, make a **90**-degree turn at the dead tree stump. (degrees)

The trailer was **14′ x 26′**. (measurements)

In the committee report, it was stated that **73**% (or **73** percent) of the proceeds went to the scholarship fund.

Some of the following sentences use numbers incorrectly. If the sentence is correct, mark a *C* next to it. If the sentence is incorrect, make the necessary changes to correct it.

1. Mary sold 4 sets of dishes and 26 dish towels for eighteen dollars and seventy-four cents in nineteen hundred and sixty-three at seven eighty-two Elm Street.

2. 11 A.M. in the morning was the time set for rehearsal.

3. The instructor's assignment was to read pages ten through fifteen before September twenty-second, nineteen hundred and seventy-seven.

4. 402 elk grazed on eight hundred acres of protected forest land.

5. The temperature of ninety-two degrees was three degrees above the previous high temperature of eighteen-hundred and ninety-two.

6. The Joneses gained back four % of their investment by June sixth, 1974.

7. Frances was explaining to her seventh grade students that the "pie" diagram gave them a visual aid in adding up to 100%.

8. By the 21st century, the population of Rerdon should reach 102, eighteen more than their current census records.

9. The morning classes at Franklin Community College began at 8 A.M. and ended at 8 P.M. in the evening.

10. The house dimensions stated in the contract were twenty-six feet by forty feet, but when the contractors finished on July twenty-second the dimensions were only 23 feet by 36 feet.

NAME _____   DATE _____

Some of the following sentences use numbers incorrectly. If the sentence is correct, mark a *C* next to it. If the sentence is incorrect, make the necessary changes to correct it.

1. The statistics show that real estate value went up 50 percent in the Blue Lake area and only thirty percent in the White Lake area.

2. The total price for the used car was $1341 and fifty cents, payable on June first nineteen hundred and seventy-nine.

3. Dean Robinson's 10:00 A.M. meeting concerning the future of the two-year colleges was cancelled.

4. Ms. Smith, who taught ninety-eight junior-high students, lives at one hundred and sixteen Aspen Way in apartment three-D.

5. Marshall found in the August 16th issue of *Solar Energy* that a sixty degree angle on a greenhouse roof would collect the most energy from the sun.

6. The garage sale at 409 White Street gave Dan 90% of what he needed for his new apartment at 16 Firth Street.

7. The minutes of the February 22nd meeting showed that 243 people attended the Cattlemen's Convention, only 75% of the membership.

8. The reforestation project estimated that they would need 84 blue spruce and 49 lodgepole pine seedlings to replant the 30 acres.

9. The gentleman in the third row asked, "Exactly how many of the 83 pages of text are necessary in our revised constitution?"

10. In my estimation, the 1000 acres would cost at least $750,000.

NAME _____ DATE _____

The following paragraph contains some errors in the usage of numbers. Make the necessary changes to correct the errors.

At Red Rock State University in Kansas, the Composition Committee met with the Curriculum Committee at 9:00 A.M. on the morning of June first and revealed several problems with the teaching of writing. The committee had discovered that seventy-three percent of the incoming freshmen had inadequate preparation for the 3 required composition courses. The 1975, 1976, and 1977 testings of 100 students showed on the average 48.5 percent of the students lacked a background in basic grammar, 31.5 percent had serious spelling deficiencies, and 20 percent could not read above the 4th grade level. Though the Curriculum Committee seemed sympathetic, they said that the forty-three English faculty are paid to "teach these students something" and that teaching writing should be their priority. If necessary, the department would have to cut down on the 18 upper division courses to allow for at least 65 sections of composition. Also it was suggested that the Composition Committee contact Composition HELP, at 926 Alameda Avenue in Seattle, Washington, and ask about the 8 or 9 specialized composition programs; perhaps one might suit the Kansas students. 2500 incoming freshmen must be helped in the Fall nineteen hundred and seventy-nine semester, and the fifteen member committee was charged with doing just that.

Mechanics

CAPITALIZATION

It is important to observe the rules governing the capitalization of certain words. Capitalize the following:

---

1 The first word of every sentence.

The students groaned at the new reading assignment.

---

2 The first letter of the first word of every line of traditional English verse.

Be careful to note the conventions followed by the poet; some poetry from the 20th century deviates from tradition.

The modest Rose puts forth a thorn:

The humble sheep, a threatening horn:

While the filly white, shall in love delight,

Nor a thorn nor a threat stain her beauty bright.

3 All nouns, pronouns, verbs, adjectives, adverbs, and first and last words of titles of publications and other artistic works.

A Conceptual Theory of Rhetoric (book)
"The Rocking Horse Winner" (short story)
Voyage of Life (painting)

4 Names

A. The first name, middle name or initial, and last name of a person, real or fictional.

J. R. Ewing   Samuel T. Coleridge
Houdini   Emma Bovary

B. Honorary and official titles when they precede the name of a person and when they are used in place of the name of a specific person.

Pope John Paul or the Pope   Queen Elizabeth or the Queen
President Reagan or the President   Senator Howard Baker or the Senator
Mom [but not my mom]   Dad [but not my dad]

5 Names of places

A. Names and abbreviations of villages, towns, cities, counties, states, nations, regions, and street names.

Toledo, Ohio   Bannock County   Fiji Islands
Sunset Boulevard   Canada   Wall Street
the Pacific Northwest   Southeast Asia   the North [but: we flew north]

B. The names of rivers, lakes, falls, oceans, mountains, deserts, and parks.

the Sawtooth Mountains   Niagara Falls
Lake Erie   Yellowstone National Park
the Pacific Ocean   the Sahara Desert

6 Names and abbreviations of businesses, industries, institutions, agencies, schools, political parties, religious denominations, and literary, philosophical, artistic movements and brand names.

Acme Plumbing
Smithsonian Institute
Central Intelligence
  Agency
University of Illinois
Catholicism

Democrats
Romantic Literature
Buddhism
Existentialism
Communism
Peter Pan peanut butter

Coca Cola
Scott, Foresman and
  Company
Toyota Corolla
American Library
  Association

7 Titles of historical events, epochs, and periods.

Renaissance
the Depression
World War I
Korean War

Ice Age
the Battle of Waterloo
the Treaty of Versailles
the Elizabethan Age

8 Names of weekdays, months, holidays, holy days, and other special days or periods.

Monday
September
Christmas Eve

Mardi Gras
Lent
National Book Week

9 Names and abbreviations of the books and divisions of the Bible and other sacred books. No italics are used for these titles (see Item 83).

Genesis
Exodus
King James Version
Book of Job

Koran
Bhagavad Gita
Vulgata
Pss. (Psalms)

NAME _____ DATE _____

Capitalize all the words that should be capitalized.

1. joe and will traveled south to atlanta, georgia after living for many years in the north.

2. he worked at the spitzer building in december and january.

3. the students read *the valley of the dolls* at johnson community college.

4. george franklin, the new counselor, liked to call his mother, "ma."

5. reverend mckay visited the president in the georgia white house.

6. my brother studied spanish, business history 202, accounting 101, and he also took courses in government and sociology.

7. the old man lived on alameda road in eastern new york during the spanish-american war.

8. during her trip to england last summer, barb visited the duke of edinburgh, stayed at buckingham palace, and fell in the loch ness.

9. the article, "creole cooking: the southern life," was published in the may issue of *town and country magazine.*

10. over and over emily screamed, "i don't believe you henry. you are a member of the ku klux klan!"

11. the local democratic rally lasted from monday through thursday, july 9 through 12.

12. the newly established publishing company, peach tree press, was founded by the faculty at georgia community college.

13. bonnie and bob's trip to the sierra desert was enjoyable.

14. state representative Smith called for a vote in the illinois legislature.

15. the mayor dedicated the northbrook library to the 1983 graduates of northbrook high school.

NAME _____ DATE _____

Capitalize all the words that should be capitalized.

1. reverend johnson read the book of job to the lakeshore women's auxiliary.

2. sarah was taken to lunch twice by mr. smith during national secretary week.

3. jennifer asked whether or not banquo in shakespeare's *macbeth* was really a ghost or merely macbeth's imagination.

4. prince charles did not take part in world war I, however, his ancestors in southhampton did.

5. henry miller resided at big sur on the california coast.

6. the book, *mansfield park* by jane austen, talks about fanny and her trials.

7. oriental literature's 303 course includes the *bhagavad gita,* poems by lao tzu, and *the tale of genji.*

8. on tuesday, april 21, senator smith from kansas proposed new legislation concerning the holidays of labor day, memorial day, and veterans' day.

9. martha asked, "does french 101 apply toward graduation requirements for a b.a. with a major in philosophy?"

10. ms. philips' new corporation, idaho's maps and guides, was formed earlier this year in april.

NAME _____   DATE _____

Proofread the following paragraph, checking for errors in capitalization.

Mr. hart arrived precisely at 10:00 to begin the introduction to english 101: freshman composition. as he rushed toward the desk, he dropped numerous sheets of his manuscript, "the influence of 17th century politics on ben jonson's literary style." Stooping to pick up his papers, he knocked one of his texts, *the little english handbook,* onto jill furman's desk. When tom potts helped mr. hart pick up his books, he noticed that the professor's rumpled jacket was from lord and taylor's department store. Finally after all the initial commotion, english 101 began. during his presentation, Mr. Hart said, "each of you freshman students must attend a weekly conference on tuesday or thursday in addition to regular class meetings on monday, wednesday, and friday. And the holidays during the semester, veterans' day, thanksgiving, and christmas, will have to be made up with extra assignments." One student angrily grumbled, "who does he think he is, the president or the pope?" Finally, at 10:50, the students filed out of the classroom. tom said to jill, "so this is life at blackrock university."

In the following passage there are errors with the use of quotation marks, numbers, hyphens, and capitalization. Find those errors and make the necessary corrections.

The wild west book club members are excited about their special offer to new members. 75 special editions of northwest passage are being offered at forty-percent discount. These copies, having leather covers and handsewn bindings, will be offered with new memberships for ninety dollars; on the regular market they sell for $150. This special edition was designed by investors especially for the book club in order to increase their membership. At present the club has nearly 500 members. 1000 members is the goal of the investors.

The book will be of interest to a wide range of academicians as well as enthusiasts of pioneer culture. Historians will find a recently discovered travel diary of Lewis and Clark from which the editors have included entries from 1804- -1805, the beginning of Lewis and Clark's northwest expedition. The chapter entitled 'Pioneer Men: lost and found' describes some of the Lewis and Clark exploits. Also the special edition includes chapters entitled "Pioneer women" and 'Indian art'. Of interest to linguists is the section on the Nez Perce Indians and their language. Here the editors have noted new elements of the language heretofore unrecorded. And of general interest are the 3 chapters on farming, family life, and gold mining. All in all, the book is the pièce de résistance of the book club series.

Since this special edition encapsulates the discovery of the northwest territory as revealed by explorers of all kinds from the pre1850 era, it could well become a classic of history treatises. The well documented evidence presents newly discovered explorers' routes which will change some theories about Indian migrations. In the concluding chapter, A look forward, the editors pose new questions that arise from their discussions. The editors have done all they could to encourage prospective buyers and to increase the membership of the wild west book club.

Research Paper

EVALUATING SOURCES, TAKING NOTES, AND DOCUMENTATION

In writing your own research paper, you will need to know about such essential preliminary research procedures as topic selection, efficient library use, and working outline and working bibliography preparation. In the following exercises, that work has already been done for you. There are five exercises in all; the first three are interrelated. You are given a specified topic: the potentially harmful effects of the close alliance between corporate business and television networks. You are also given five possible sources of information on that topic. Your task, in the first three exercises, is (1) to evaluate the five sources for relevance and reliability, (2) to take notes on the sources you find to be relevant and reliable, and (3) to write a paragraph in which you incorporate your notes. In the fourth exercise, you are asked to construct MLA style Endnote and Bibliography pages from a list of ten sources. In the fifth exercise, you will construct APA style entries for a *References* page.

Evaluation of Sources

In the initial stages of any research paper project, you should become familiar with how to use the library, you should limit your topic and prepare a working outline of the points you want to cover in your essay, and you should prepare a working bibliography of titles which seem to be useful.

After you have compiled a representative list of potentially useful sources, you can gather them. But before you begin to read and take notes, you must evaluate your sources for relevance and reliability. That is, before you spend time reading large portions of a text, you need to use a method whereby you can tell almost at a glance if that text contains information you can use and if that information is reliable.

1 Relevance

To check a source for relevance, ask yourself two questions: (1) does the source contain information related to any of the subtopics you will cover in your essay (your working outline will provide you with a list of those subtopics) and (2) does the source contain the kind of information you wish to use?

A. The first question can be answered in various ways depending on whether the source is a book-length study or a shorter article. If you are evaluating a book, check the table of contents and the index for a list of topics covered. Sometimes, however, the table of contents and index are not very helpful in enabling you to understand exactly what the book covers. In that case, read the preface, introduction, and conclusion to the book. These are usually very short and can be read in a few minutes. If those sections aren't helpful, don't give up on the book. Turn next to the introductory paragraphs of each chapter and just skim them.

   If you are evaluating a periodical article or short essay, read the introduction and conclusion. Sometimes writers of journal articles supply headings to announce the topic of a particular section of the article. Check those. And finally, read the topic sentences of the various paragraphs to determine what material is covered.

B. The second question about the kind of information a source contains can be answered by a quick glance at the chapter, section, or paragraphs which contain information on your subject. If you want factual information in the form of statistics, experiments, or case studies, you can tell at a glance whether the source you are evaluating contains such information or whether it contains only the general opinions of the author.

2 Reliability

If a source contains information relevant to your purposes, you must still evaluate it for reliability. To check for reliability, ask yourself: what is the source of information?

To answer this question, check such things as the credentials and/or reputation of the author, the reputation of the publisher, the critical reception of the source, the quality of the research behind the writing, and the date the source was published or printed.

No single element will automatically disqualify a source as unreliable; you must use your judgment. For example, if you were writing an essay with an antimilitary slant, you should not automatically assume that all publications of the Department of Defense would be unreliable. Those publications might provide you with statistics you can use to support your arguments. So, as is the case with relevance, reliability is most often determined by your needs. If information published in 1950 is useful to you, then the source should not be considered unreliable on the basis that it is outdated. However, if you need current information, then a source published in 1950 should be considered unreliable.

The same is true of the credentials and/or reputation of the author. An author can possess solid credentials and an excellent reputation and still produce work that is unreliable for your purposes; or an author might not have established a reputation at all and still produce a work that is reliable. You would decide on reliability or unreliability based on what kind of information is presented, how the information is presented, and whether or not you detect that a writer's bias might affect the information presented. If an author with solid credentials presents opinions on an emotional issue without providing details to support those opinions, and if that author shows an obvious bias toward one side of an issue, you might question the reliability of the source.

There are several ways for you to check for reliability.

(1) Note the publication date, the publisher, the extensiveness of the bibliography used by the author, the kind of evidence the author uses in the text, and the information given in a book or periodical about the author (if any is given).
(2) Check an author's credentials by looking in one of several biographical reference books such as *Who's Who in America*.
(3) Check the critical reception of a book source by looking up a review of the book in *Book Review Digest* or another book review index.
(4) Learn to identify (by consulting your instructor or a librarian, and by experience) the most reputable publishing houses and learn not only to distinguish between scholarly journals and popular magazines but also to be aware that periodicals can have editorial biases.

While the process of evaluation sounds time consuming, once you know what to look for and where to look, evaluation of a source is quite simple.

Assume you are writing a research paper examining some of the problems brought on by the popularity of television. One of the points you wish to make is that the substantial investment of big business interests in television in the form of advertisements creates an unhealthy alliance. You want to point out (1) that money spent on commercials and money generated by commercials is substantial and (2) that as a result advertisers can control programming in potentially negative ways.

Remember you are not interested in speculation but in factual information in the form of figures and case studies or examples.

On the next few pages, you are given information about and from five different sources. Of those sources, three of the five are particularly relevant and reliable, given your purpose. Carefully examine the information and note whether that information indicates that the source will be Useful or Not Useful.

After you have done this for all five sources, make a judgment about which three of the five are relevant and reliable overall. Then write a short essay (300–500 words) explaining your decision. In your essay be sure to refer to the following:

1) The kind of information contained in the source (assume the selections provided are representative);
2) The date of publication of the information (discuss whether the date is relevant or not);
3) The critical reception of the source (where applicable);
4) The author's credentials (where given);
5) The publisher of the source.

TELEVISION FRAUD

THE HISTORY AND IMPLICATIONS OF THE QUIZ SHOW SCANDALS

Kent Anderson   764785

Contributions in American Studies, Number 39

GREENWOOD PRESS

WESTPORT, CONNECTICUT • LONDON, ENGLAND

Library of Congress Cataloging in Publication Data

Anderson, Kent.
  Television Fraud.

  (Contributions in American studies ; no. 39 ISSN: 0084-9227)
  Based on the author's thesis, University of Washington.
  Bibliography: p
  Includes index.
  1. Quiz shows—United States. 2. Fraud—United States. I. Title.
PN1992.8.Q5A5   791.45′7   77-94755
ISBN 0-313-20321-0

Library of Congress Catalog Card Number: 77-94755
ISBN: 0-313-20321-0
ISSN: 0084-9227

First published in 1978

Greenwood Press, Inc.
51 Riverside Avenue, Westport, Connecticut 06880

Printed in the United States of America
10 9 8 7 6 5 4 3 2 1

About the Author

Kent Anderson was awarded the Ph.D. in history by
the University of Washington in 1975.

CONTENTS

III. THE TEXT

A. Preface (Representative Page)

society, produced a public empathy and fascination that swept the nation. Closely related to this was the question of what constituted an educated person in America. Did most television viewers of the quizzes perceive the successful contestants as well educated, wise, or merely well trained? The nature of the knowledge that spewed forth from the quizzes was a source of consternation to many educators, serious television critics, and societal commentators who resented the application of dollar signs as reward for snippets and bits of knowledge devoid of having demonstrated any evidence of reasoning from those who supplied it and who thought the entire process represented a debasement of accumulating knowledge for its own sake. Another body of opinion held the big-money shows more in wonder than in scorn. Some teachers hoped that the shows increased the motivation for learning in youngsters, while other critics viewed the programs in truly positive fashion laden with worthwhile and heroic personages.[2]

Since this is a story about commercial television, the institution of American advertising figures prominently. The responsibility of advertising for what occurred is debatable only by degree. The late David M. Potter once said that the primary influence exerted by the institution of advertising was not upon our economical system but rather upon the values of our society.[3] This study looks at that supposition. Advertising is but one large component in the business process, however; others explored in some detail here are the television industry and its regulatory bodies, the Federal Trade Commission and the Federal Communications Commission. (In fact it could be argued that this study is more a business history than a social history, but the reader will make that determination.)

The ideas and areas of American study thus far discussed were reflected in varying degrees in the short-lived institution of the big-money quiz show. Had there been no subsequent scandal connected with these shows, their study still would

B. Excerpt from Conclusion

CONCLUSION

Why did the fixed quizzes occur? Much of the reasoning must be economic. Meyer Weinberg emphasizes this cause. He showed that Geritol's annual sales jumped from $10,482,000 in 1956 (before *Twenty-one* began) to $13,975,000 in 1957 and $12,379,000 in 1958, when the show was on the air. They fell to $10,600,000 when it was cancelled. Geritol sales, then were approximately 25 percent higher while *Twenty-one* was being aired. Geritol did not interfere with the quiz's workings, nor was *Twenty-one* a huge success in the ratings. For Revlon and *The $64,000 Question*, the figures are even more impressive. Before 1955, when the first big-money quiz was aired, Revlon's annual average net profit (1950–54) was $1,200,000. From 1955 to 1958 it rose to $7,680,000 and averaged $11,078,996 in the years 1959 and 1960. Money, according to Weinberg, was the prime motivating factor for producers to arrange the outcome of quizzes they hoped would increase the ratings and, in turn, the sponsor's profits and interest in remaining with the show. Revlon demonstrated a strong relationship between television ratings and sales, but this correlation did not exist for many other shows.

There is more to the meaning of the quiz frauds than saying that they demonstrate the avarice of American corporations linked with advertising agencies and the television industry. There is more significance to the scandals than proving a theory of materialistic determinism even though greed, arguably, may have been the most prevalent human behavioral trait displayed throughout this entire tale.

From the viewpoint of the contestants, the monetary lure was reason enough for many to deceive, but other factors also fig-

IV. INDEX (REPRESENTATIVE PAGE)

V. BIBLIOGRAPHY (REPRESENTATIVE PAGE)

PUBLIC DOCUMENTS

Congressional Index, 1959-1960. New York: Commerce Clearing House, 1960. Vol. 1.

Congressional Quarterly Almanac. 86th Cong., 2d sess. Washington: Congressional Quarterly, 1960.

U.S. Congress. House. Committee on Interstate and Foreign Commerce. *Communications Act Amendments, 1960.* H. Rept. 1800, to Accompany S. 1898, 86th Cong., 2d sess., 1960.

————. *Investigation of Regulatory Commissions and Agencies.* H. Rept. 1258, 86th Cong., 2d sess., 1960.

————. *Investigation of Television Quiz Shows.* Hearings before a subcommittee of the Committee on Interstate and Foreign Commerce, House of Representatives, 86th Cong., 1st sess., 1959.

BOOKS

Agnew, Clark, and O'Brien, Neil. *Television Advertising.* New York: McGraw-Hill Book Company, 1958.

Brooks, John. *The Great Leap.* New York: Harper and Row, 1968.

Brown, Les. *Television: The Business Behind the Box.* New York: Harcourt Brace Jovanovich, 1971.

Evans, Jacob. *Selling and Promoting Radio and Television.* New York: Printers' Ink Publishing Company, 1954.

Friendly, Fred W. *Due to Circumstances Beyond Our Control.* New York: Vintage Books, 1967.

Goldman, Eric F. *The Crucial Decade—and After: America, 1945-1960.* New York: Vintage Books, 1960

Hickok, Eliza Merrill. *Quiz Kids.* Boston: Houghton Mifflin, 1947.

James, William. *Memories and Studies.* New York: Longmans, Green and Company, 1912.

Kando, Thomas M. *Leisure and Popular Culture in Transition.* St. Louis: C. V. Mosby Company, 1975.

Potter, David M. *People of Plenty.* Chicago: University of Chicago, Press, 1954.

Schlesinger, Arthur M., Jr. "Sources of the New Deal." In *Paths of American Thought,* edited by Arthur M. Schlesinger, Jr. and Morton White. Boston: Houghton Mifflin, 1963.

Weinberg, Meyer. *TV in America.* New York: Ballantine Books, 1962.

ARTICLES

Ace, Goodman. "The $64,000 Answer." *Saturday Review,* August 13, 1955, p. 23.

"Admen Face the TV Issue." *Business Week,* November 21, 1959, pp. 116-117

VI. BOOK REVIEWS

BOOK REVIEW DIGEST 1980

ANDERSON, KENT. Television fraud; the history and implications of the quiz show scandals. (Contributions in Am. studies, no39) 226p $18.95 '78 Greenwood Press
791.45   Quiz shows.   Fraud

"On Tuesday evening, June 7, 1955, at 10:00 p.m., The $64,000 question appeared for the first time. This quiz program . . . [grew in popularity until it] was cancelled on November 4, 1958, after having given away $2,106,000 in prize money and 29 Cadillacs. This book documents the story of The $64,000 question, the 44 quiz and game shows it spawned, the subsequent 'scandal without precedence' connected with these shows, and the . . . fraud involved in the preparation of contestants. The book also examines the influence of advertising on the economic system and societal values; it comments on the uses of leisure time in America; and it details public apathy in the wake of the scandals." (Choice) Bibliography. Index.

"The evolution of the quiz show mania is intriguing, but Kent Anderson rightly believes that it is more important to understand the public response to the scandals that erupted in 1958. Unfortunately, this is the book's weakest point. Anderson only partly succeeds in using the scandals as a litmus test of the American character. Television Fraud suffers from the academic condition of premature publication, and this slender little volume is conceptually sketchy and based solely on published sources. It does not really tell us anything new. . . . To his credit, Anderson avoided muckraking, but his uncertainty about whether his book 'is more a business history than a social history' remains a question this reviewer is unable to answer." E. V. Toy

Am Hist R 84:1500 D '79 550w

"Anderson gives an excellent chronological survey of the quiz show mania from 1955 to date. Well-written, the book is almost exciting to read; the research is comprehensive; each chapter is followed by numerous references; and the book includes a six-page bibliography. Although one speculates why such a book did not immediately follow the quiz show scandals of the middle 50s, the book will interest both reminiscing older readers and the students undertaking historical research."

Choice 16:522 Je '79 210w

"The author of this study has been limited in his research to a few books, testimony taken in a few days of congressional hearings, and the culling of a couple of volumes of the Readers' Guide to Periodical Literature, presumably because corporate records were inaccessible and surviving participants withheld cooperation. Nonetheless, the author provides a clearly told story of the rise and decline of the television quiz programs. . . . Too briefly treated are the 'implications' promised in the title: a national character shaped by advertising; a work ethic as unintended inspiration for the quizzes; unrestrained consumerism; and low broadcast standards tolerated by a weak Federal Communications Commission. These implications also include viewers made powerless by network oligopoly; apathetic or timid or cynical journalists . . . and the claim that the scandals helped break the hold of sponsors on programming. All of these implications are taken up to some extent, but each deserves elaboration that would lead to fuller understanding of the place of television in recent American history." Thomas Cripps

J Am Hist 66:988 Mr '80 350w

TELEVISION

A Selection of Readings from TV Guide® Magazine

Edited by Barry G. Cole

52457

CONTRIBUTORS

RICHARD S. SALANT has been President of CBS News since 1966.
Before becoming a director of CBS in 1961, Mr. Salant was an attorney
for the United States Government and a Vice President of CBS Incorporated.

from *Who's Who in America*

SALANT, RICHARD S., broadcasting co. exec.; b. N.Y.C., Apr. 14, 1914; s. Louis
and Florence (Aronson) S.; A.B., Harvard U., 1935, LL.B., 1938. Admitted to
N.Y. bar, 1938; atty. U.S. Govt., 1938-43; asso. Rosenman, Goldmark, Colin &
Kaye, 1946-48, partner, 1948-52; v.p. CBS Inc., 1952-61, dir., 1961-68, pres. CBS
News, 1961-64, 64-79, v.p. CBS Inc., 1964-66; vice chmn. NBC Inc., 1979—, also dir.
Served to lt. comdr. USNR, 1943-46. Office: 30 Rockefeller Plaza New York NY
10020

II. TABLE OF CONTENTS (SELECTIONS)

III. THE TEXT

A. Preface (Representative Page)

PREFACE

Despite an increase in the number of books and articles concerning commercial television, there has been no single collection of readings designed to provide an overview of today's medium: that is, the content of television, how information about the audience is obtained and used, television's role and its significance in society, and its regulation and control. This consideration, along with my conviction, shared by many of my colleagues, that much of the most significant material about television has appeared in TV GUIDE, provided the impetus for this volume.

This book, therefore, has a dual purpose. First, to make readily available some of the important writing about contemporary commercial television from TV GUIDE; second, to at least partially fulfill the need for a basic reader in television which will be of benefit to both the layman and the college student of broadcasting and communications.

Throughout, I have attempted to keep editing to a minimum. I have updated information in footnotes and in the introductions when I thought it useful. It has occasionally been advisable to delete material from individual articles when the material was dated or when the subject was covered in greater detail and more appropriately placed in other portions of the book. These deletions are formally noted.

Some of the more lengthy articles included in this collection were originally published as separate parts in two or more issues of TV GUIDE. In some cases these divisions were eliminated while in other instances material reviewing earlier parts of the article were deleted and the divisions were kept intact.

The articles are not reproduced in chronological order and thus there are many apparent inconsistencies in the titles of industry personnel. The references to executives and personnel are so numerous, however, that in most instances I felt it inadvisable to tamper with

v

B. Representative Passage

He Has Exercised His Right to Be Wrong

By Richard Salant

SEPTEMBER 15, 1969

Federal Communications Commissioner Nicholas Johnson's article in TV GUIDE is shocking, if true. It is just as shocking if it is not true. And as it relates to CBS News, it most certainly is not true.

Commissioner Johnson claims that, for economic reasons, broadcasters withhold information and suppress discussion of issues vital to Americans. Therefore, he concludes broadcasters are hypocritically concerned about government censorship since the real evil is self-censorship arising out of broadcaster timidity and economic self-protection.

Much of Commissioner Johnson's article relates to broadcast journalism. To the extent that Commissioner Johnson deals with entertainment, I will leave to those responsible for that programming the task of examining Commissioner Johnson's accuracy, although the inaccuracy of his charges against television journalism necessarily raises serious questions about the rest of his charges.

But I can speak only in respect of broadcast journalism—and only for CBS News. And for CBS News, I state flatly that Commissioner Johnson is totally, completely, 100 percent wrong—on all counts.

Let me start with the most general aspect of Johnson's frightening world of fantasy.

In the 11 years I was a CBS corporate officer and in the six years that I have been president of CBS News, to my knowledge there is no issue, no topic, no story, which CBS News has ever been forbidden, or instructed directly or indirectly, to cover or not to cover, by corporate management. Corporate management at CBS has scrupulously observed that vital doctrine of separation of powers without which honest journalism cannot thrive—the separation between the corporation and an autonomous news organization.

Second, the separation between CBS News and the sales departments of the CBS radio and television networks and their advertisers

330

has been complete. CBS News has no sales department. Its function *331*
is to choose the topics and stories and to prepare the broadcasts; the
sales departments and the advertisers play no part in that process. No
topic has ever been selected or omitted, and no treatment has ever
been affected, by the imagined or expressed wishes of an advertiser.
Long since, the policy has been established that CBS News makes
the broadcasts and the advertiser makes and sells his products, and
never the twain shall meet.

Third, there has been no *self*-censorship: I—and to the best of my
knowledge, my associates at CBS News—have never avoided a topic
or altered treatment to protect, or to avoid displeasing, corporate
management or any advertiser. As I have stated, anybody in the organization who avoided a topic or distorted his normal judgments in the
treatment of a topic in order to avoid offending the economic interests
of any advertisers, or to please CBS management, would thereby
betray his professional heritage and would disqualify himself from
working with CBS News.

So much for the general principles. As far as I have gone to this
point, the issue between Commissioner Johnson and me is, to the
outsider, bound to be inconclusive: It is his work against mine, and
I would not blame any third party who knows neither of us for giving
the nod to the Commissioner, since I have a personal stake in my own
reputation and the reputation of my CBS News associates and he at
least *appears* to be a responsible, neutral government official with the
public interest at heart. So let us turn to each of the specific charges
of suppression and avoidance which Commissioner Johnson advances
to prove his general thesis. Taking them one at a time, the record
shows he is wrong all along the line. His batting average turns out to
be .000. At most, he proves himself to be a pitcher with more speed
than control, rather than a hitter.

Item: Commissioner Johnson writes that "We have been shown
miles of film from Vietnam, it is true. But how much has television
told you about the multi-billion dollar corporate profits from that
war?"

Plenty. We have included in our broadcasts the stories of Viet-
namese corruption, of the operations of American business firms in
Vietnam, and of war contractor costs. Example: Congressman Pike's
disclosure of the sale to the Defense Department of $210 worth of
generator knobs for $33,000. Example: A two-part report in June
1969 on Pentagon waste and overruns.

Index

595

V. BIBLIOGRAPHY

None Available

VI. BOOK REVIEWS

None Available

I. AUTHOR, EDITOR, PUBLISHER

SOURCE 3

BusinessWeek

Readers report

Cooperation, not confrontation

I think every manager should read "Concessionary bargaining: Will the new cooperation last?" (Labor, June 14) very carefully. As a professional arbitrator, I feel that the adversary confrontations of past years must be replaced by wide-

[...]

incurred by our subsidiary Trans-Dyn, is totally unrelated to those losses. It was, in fact, paid in 1981 to one of Trans-Dyn's customers so that the customer might compensate the company for

1978 losses incurred by Trans-Dyn (since reorganized) on four large wastewater projects. Moreover, of the 20 companies acquired by Dynalectron since 1969, 18 are retained as of this date, only two of which have produced operational losses.

Your statement that the company has "already collected $85 million on its technology from a pilot plant in Catlettsburg" is incorrect. Pilot-plant-related revenue and supporting laboratory work

[...]

pension plan to maintain actuarial equivalence of the lump-sum option with the basic monthly pension. Other bargaining units of the Oil, Chemical & Atomic Workers outside the Port Arthur (Tex.)

Editor-in-Chief	Lewis H. Young
Editor	John L. Cobbs
Managing editor	John A. Dierdorff
Deputy editor	William Wolman
Asst. managing editor	John Maughan
Senior editors	Robert W. Henkel, Richard F. Janssen, Daniel D. McCrary, John E. Pluenneke, Sally Powell, Alice L. Priest, Seymour Zucker
Senior writers	Jack Patterson, John Pearson, Sol W. Sanders, Morton A. Reichek, Stewart Toy, Brenton Welling
Art director	John R. Vogler
Senior systems mgr.	Richard I. Ulman
Associate editors	Sheila Cunningham, Jane H. Cutaia, Robin Grossman, John Hoerr, Ephraim Lewis, Bruce Nussbaum, Otis Port, E. Roy Ray, Joseph L. Wiltsee

Publisher	J. R. Pierce
Associate Publisher	Edward B. Hughes
DIRECTOR, MARKETING COMMUNICATIONS	Donald J. Austermann
RESEARCH & DEVELOPMENT DIRECTOR	John J. Bedell
INTERNATIONAL PUBLISHING DIRECTOR	Denis C. Beran
NEW PRODUCT DEVELOPMENT DIRECTOR	John E. Cortissoz
ADVERTISING DEVELOPMENT DIRECTOR	H. Sherman Davis
CIRCULATION DIRECTOR	Kenneth R. Graham
CONTROLLER	Joseph M.G. Huber
ADVERTISING BUSINESS DIRECTOR	Alton C. Lynch
PUBLIC RELATIONS DIRECTOR	Mary C. McGeachy
INTERNATIONAL ADVERTISING DIRECTOR	Earl S. Moore Jr.
PRODUCTION DIRECTOR	John E. Thompson

II. TABLE OF CONTENTS

Business Week (ISSN 0007-7135) published weekly, except for one issue in January, by McGraw-Hill, Inc. U. S. subscriber rate $34.95 per year. In Canada, one year: CDN $49.95. Single copies, $2.00. Executive, Editorial, Circulation, and Advertising Offices: McGraw-Hill Building, 1221 Avenue of the Americas, New York, N.Y. 10020. Second-class postage paid at New York, N.Y., and at additional mailing offices. Postage paid at Montreal, P.Q. Title Reg. in U.S. Patent Office. Postmaster: Please send Form 3579 to BUSINESS WEEK, P. O. Box 430, Hightstown, N.J. 08520. Argentina: Clasificada por el Correo Argentino como de "interes general" bajo tarifa postal reducida. Concesion No. 873.

BUSINESS WEEK: July 26, 1982   1

III. THE TEXT

MEDIA & ADVERTISING

Prime time gets even costlier

"For national advertisers, network TV is still the only game in town," explains one advertising agency executive whose clients may have to pay higher prices for smaller prime-time audiences next season. With the demand for such time growing, industry experts believe that network advertising revenues could rise to $5 billion this year from about $4.4 billion in 1981. "That would be a very respectable increase in a period when inflation is running at about 6%," says Anthony Hoffman, a vice-president at A. G. Becker Inc. Advertising executives say that a 30-second commercial on a top-rated show such as ABC's *Love Boat* or *Fantasy Island* could jump from $120,000 to about $134,000 or more, and the price of a spot on less popular shows would rise from $65,000 to $73,000.

Even with the uncertain economy, many advertisers such as food and beer manufacturers are likely to raise their budgets as much as 14% or 15%. Movie companies, which spend about $115 million on network TV last year, are expected to spend as much as $150 million this year. And the soft drink wars between Pepsi-Cola and Coca-Cola will be backed by heavy TV campaigns.

Lost audience. At the same time, the audience for prime-time TV is dwindling. According to A. C. Nielsen Co., there has been a drop in the percentage of homes watching network TV from 52% in 1977 for the three networks to 48.9% in the fall of 1981. Even more significant has been the 14% decline in the number of women viewers, aged 18 to 49, in that same five-year period. Indications are that younger people are watching more independent stations as well as pay television. "Many are watching stations such as

Networks traditionally guarantee advertisers either households or target audiences, especially women viewers. Last season all three, but particularly troubled NBC, had to make good—that is, give advertisers additional time later in the season to compensate them for failure to meet guarantees. Reportedly, NBC had to make good so many minutes in the first quarter of 1982 that it had very little inventory to sell. As a result, advertisers had to go to ABC and CBS for "scatter time"—commercial time sold after the season is under way—only to find that prices had gone up 20%.

The networks are taking a tougher stance on audience guarantees. Says NBC's Aaron Cohen, vice-president for national sales: "Our research shows us there is a potential for a small decline this season." And CBS is refusing to guarantee advertisers target audiences.

Media buyers, who begin making "upfront buys"—reserving time on the networks' prime-time schedules—in early July, say that deals for the fall season are taking longer to conclude. One agency executive says: "The networks are asking for more money to compensate for the decline in viewers. That makes negotiations very difficult."

Home Box Office that don't run commercials," grouses one media buyer. "That audience is a nonrecoupable loss." Concedes Leonard Sass, vice-president of corporate network TV services at Kenyon & Eckhardt Inc.: "Demographics have gone to hell in a bucket."

Rumors persist on Madison Avenue that one agency, Batten, Barton, Durstine & Osborn Inc., has already written off CBS in its upfront buys for Pepsi-Cola and Wrigley's gum, because CBS was demanding an 18% increase. The agency did place its upfront buys with ABC and NBC. "It will be a brutal buying season," says one media buyer.

With the erosion of network audiences, some advertisers have turned to the independent stations that syndicate reruns of successful programs such as *M*A*S*H*. In 1981 revenues rose 24% for independents, compared with a 13% increase for network affiliates. But the 165 independent stations reach only 76% of all U.S. households. And even the successful *Merv Griffin Show*, which runs on Metromedia's WNEW-TV in New York, attracts a 5 rating compared with an average 15 rating for a competing prime-time network broadcast.

Most efficient buy. "For national advertisers the network buy is still extremely efficient," says one agency executive, "and it is also more practical for the advertising agency. One executive can handle $50 million work of network TV, but it takes a large staff to buy spot TV—placing national advertisers on local stations—because you have to deal with some many different stations."

Cable TV advertising revenues are soaring, but they are still minuscule relative to those of the networks. Industry expert Paul Kagan projects that they will reach $251 million this year, a 95% increase over 1981. Still, only two advertiser-supported services, Ted Turner's Cable News Network and WTBS-TV, his Atlanta "superstation," have potential audiences large enough to warrant regular ratings reports from Nielsen. Without ratings, agencies have no hard data on audience size, and major advertisers are unwilling to gamble huge sums on the unknown.

With more than a month of negotiations between the agencies and the networks remaining, buying patterns are barely beginning to emerge. Indications are that despite smaller audiences and the networks' tougher stance on guarantees, advertisers will have to go where the action is. And that means spending more on network shows. ∎

IV. INDEX

None Available

V. BIBLIOGRAPHY

None Available

VI. BOOK REVIEWS

None Available

NEWTON N. MINOW

EQUAL TIME;

The Private Broadcaster
and
The Public Interest /

48385

EDITED BY LAWRENCE LAURENT

ATHENEUM
NEW YORK
1964

A. About the Editor

LAWRENCE LAURENT

Lawrence Laurent has been the television-radio editor and columnist for the *Washington Post* since 1953 and is also chairman of the editorial board of *Television Quarterly*. He holds the rank of Professorial Lecturer at The American University in Washington, D.C., teaching programing in both broadcast media. Mr. Laurent contributed to *Television's Impact on American Culture* and to *The Eighth Art* published in 1956 and 1962 respectively. For more than a decade he has covered virtually every investigation or hearing on communications, in the Congress and at the Federal Communications Commission. From the Washington Newspaper Guild he received a Front Page Award for his interpretative coverage of the 1963 hearings on audience ratings which were held before the House Special Subcommittee on Investigations.

B. About the Author

II. TABLE OF CONTENTS

CONTENTS

III. THE TEXT

A. Excerpts from the Introduction

its continuity. And as I looked into their cold slitted eyes, I knew I was fighting a losing fight; because as they told me, the Crest story is very important.

"And I agreed that the Crest story was very important, but I wondered why it wasn't advertised, for example: Tonight, eight o'clock, we present the Crest Story.

"They didn't do that. They say: We present *'What Makes Sammy Run?'*

"The strange thing about television is that the Crest Story is really more important, and the drama is something that goes in between the commercials, and will be sacrificed at any given time for that purpose."

Sponsor interference has been with us for a long time. Fred Allen once told the story about his attempt to use a joke based on the "Call for Philip Morris" slogan. Allen's punch line was to have a man answer the bellboy (a corporate character for the tobacco company) and to be told, "You've just been drafted." An account executive, representing the advertising agency that handled Mr. Allen's own pharmaceutical sponsor and a rival cigarette brand, didn't get the joke. He suggested a change: "Make it 'Call for Lucky Strike.'" Allen sighed and recalled, "He never did see the difference."

In the television age of 1962 a superior dramatic actor, Lee J. Cobb, went West to take a continuing role in a series called "The Virginian." In working up the part, Cobb decided that his explosive, irascible character needed to chew and puff a cigar; in stepped a production executive and said this character bit just would not do. "After all," it was explained, "we might land a cigarette sponsor."

One of television's finest writers, Rod Serling, has also recounted the changes in a script that an advertising agency can force. Mr. Serling had based a one-hour drama on the lynching of a Negro boy in the deep South. By the time the agency had finished with the story, the chief character was a former convict, living in what one could decide was New England.

These incidents, which can be multiplied by the hundreds, show how under our present system broadcasters often abandon their own judgments and their creative people to an advertiser or his agency. The advertiser is not licensed or required to serve the public interest. Often when a broadcaster abdicates to the advertiser, the private interest takes priority over the public interest.

The creative writer who turns to television drama will meet frustration many times. Automobile sponsors do not like shows involving automobile accidents; or even stories that use "chase" scenes with cars driven at high speed to the sound of squealing brakes. Detective Michael Shayne might be an authority on cognac, but if he discusses this specialty, no beer company wants sponsorship.

Sherlock Holmes' love of the pipe rules out a cigarette company or a cigar maker for sponsorship. A coffee sponsor would not allow the comic scenes in "Gunsmoke" in which Chester makes such dreadful coffee for Marshal Matt Dillon. A company manufacturing shaving tools would never permit a bearded hero, and a soap company does not want a hero who wears dirty clothes.

Above all, writers such as Serling and Reginald Rose have complained that most sponsors want only happy stories about happy people. One large company commissioned a consumer study that tended to prove that a "low level of involvement" for the viewer was best for the sponsor. After all, if one is really involved deeply in a dramatic story, he resents the interruption from the sponsor. One producer told the FCC that sponsors "want a strong, hard-hitting, fascinating, dramatic show

INDEX

V. BIBLIOGRAPHY

None Available

VI. BOOK REVIEWS

BOOK REVIEW DIGEST 1965

MINOW, NEWTON N. Equal time; the private broadcaster and the public interest; ed. by Lawrence Laurent. 316p $5.95 Atheneum pubs.
  384.55   Television broadcasting.   U.S. Federal Communications
  Commission   64-22102
The chairman of the Federal Communications Commission during the Kennedy Administration started a national dialogue over the proper role of television in American society. The editor of this volume states that he decided "to permit Mr. Minow to speak for himself, using edited versions of the speeches that created and kept alive the first great public dialogue about American broadcasting. In the editing I have frequently omitted Mr. Minow's warm humor and ad-lib remarks for the particular occasion, but I have preserved the substantive thrust of his addresses. I have added introductory notes, explaining the settings and the circumstances of each speech, and generally some follow-up commentary to enable the reader better to assess the impact of the speeches." (Editor's note) Index.

"[The speeches] are well edited by Lawrence Laurent, radio-television editor of the Washington Post, who not only describes in exact detail the context in which each speech was delivered but supplies some very vigorous comment of his own. Mr. Minow's tone is witty and urbane, but also candid and straightforward. He does not pull his punches, yet he does not speak with hostility toward the networks. Indeed, in retrospect it is rather astonishing that the broadcasters should have been so scandalized by what he said." William Barrett
Atlantic 214:158 D '64 480w
"When [Minow] left the FCC he had accomplished, almost single-handed, one of the great feats in American public life in recent decades. He had roused the public to its claim on the broadcasting industry—and he had scared the industry into conspicuous gestures in the public interest. The story is in this book, which reveals as much about the peculiar problems of our democratic-capitalist culture as does any other book of the last 20 years. . . . Most of the programs we watch have been viewed, 'approved' and 'corrected' in advance—not by the FCC, which has never had such power, but by their sponsors. . . . As a remedy, or at least a palliative, Mr. Minow urges 'the magazine-concept' which divorces the advertiser from the program. . . . Mr. Minow's other proposals for making the TV wasteland green and fertile are not so encouraging. . . . As we follow Mr. Minow's able argument for the proliferation of stations and programs—all so thoroughly in the spirit of our competitive, abundant economy—we cannot fail to ask whether he is not simply prescribing for us more of the disease we are trying to cure." D. J. Boorstin
Book Week p4 N 29 '64 2650w
"Since the addresses were originally pepared for different audiences, much of the material is necessarily repetitious, though never boring and often controversial. . . . This is an important contribution to the generally lacklustre literature of broadcasting and is highly recommended." R. A. Hamm
Library J 89:4556 N 15 '64 160w

"What Mr. Minow sought at the F.C.C. he seeks further in this book. It is a spirited and thoughtful contribution to that continuing public dialogue without which none of our democratic institutions, and broadcasting least of all, can long remain active and healthy. This is the book's great merit, and it is for this, above all, that one wishes it wide circulation. . . . The defects of the book must be frankly faced. . . . Some of the chapters are somewhat dated. And like any book composed of speeches, this one lacks continuity and design. . . . Mr. Minow's subjects are all important. His treatment of several lacks depth. Moreover, perhaps the most important chapter (a defense of our regulatory system of broadcasting) has already appeared in another book. . . . During most of his tenure of office, Mr. Minow lacked majority support on the commission. His scope for action was limited and he was forced to resort to speechmaking. But at the end a majority was back of him." C. A. Siepmann
N Y Times Bk R p52 Ja 17 '65 700w

THE REFERENCE SHELF   VOLUME 33 NUMBER 6

TELEVISION AND RADIO

EDITED BY POYNTZ TYLER

739749

THE H. W. WILSON COMPANY

NEW YORK   1961

THE REFERENCE SHELF

The books in this series reprint articles, excerpts from books, and addresses on current issues, social trends, and other aspects of American life, and occasional surveys of foreign countries. There are six separately bound numbers in each volume, all of which are generally published in the same calendar year. One number is a collection of recent speeches on a variety of subjects; each of the remaining numbers is devoted to a single subject and gives background information and discussion from varying points of view, followed by a comprehensive bibliography.

Subscribers to the current volume receive the books as issued. The subscription rate is $10 ($12 foreign) for a volume of six numbers. The price of single numbers is $2.50 each.

PRINTED IN THE UNITED STATES OF AMERICA

II. TABLE OF CONTENTS

CONTENTS

III. THE TEXT

A. Preface

PREFACE

A television executive, beset on all sides by criticism of his industry, likes to tell detractors of the little girl who was entertaining the rector while her mother prepared tea. "Can you recite the Lord's Prayer, my dear?" he asked. The little girl recited the Lord's Prayer. "Can you recite the Apostles' Creed?" The little girl recited the Apostles' Creed. "And can you recite the Catechism?" he asked. "Look, Reverend," said the little girl. "I'm *only* seven."

Perhaps youth does account for the shortcomings of broadcasting, for radio is scarcely forty years old and television less than twenty, but some critics assert that radio became senile before it ever grew up and that television gets worse with the years.

This book makes no claim to resolve the question of broadcasting's success or failure. It simply presents the findings and the views of thoughtful men in the hope that these views, from both within and without the industry, will guide and encourage the reader to arrive at his own conclusions. To those men and their publishers the editor is grateful for permission to reprint their work.

POYNTZ TYLER

November 1961

B. Representative Passage

For the most striking aspect of TV's plight is that the economics of broadcasting, as presently organized, run directly counter to the basic law that governs the industry.

Gargantua Takes Over

Detailed figures on the finances of television are not easy to come by, but even a sampling of those available shows how the industry grew.

As recently as 1949 the networks and the fourteen stations they owned outright had modest revenues of $19.3 million and showed a loss of $12.1 million for the year. The other eighty-four television stations combined had total revenues of only $15 million and reported to the FCC aggregate losses of $13.5 million. In 1958, by contrast, some 520 stations, practically all affiliated with the networks by then, grossed more than $1.25 *billion,* realized profits estimated at $170 million before taxes, employed about thirty thousand people, and were able to show a 17 per cent return as compared with the 12 per cent average for American industry. That is an impressive nine-year record for any industry. Of the total gross revenues, moreover, the three networks and the fifteen stations they owned outright in 1958 accounted for fully 44 per cent.

Of those who keep the screen aglow, the biggest spenders are the food companies, which laid out $109.2 million in 1958 to promote their goodies, from coffier coffee to instant dog food. Next in the order of their patronage of the arts via television came the makers of toiletries and toilet goods, $98.9 million; smoking materials, $62 million; medicine and patent medicines, $58 million; automotive accessories and equipment, $52.5 million. The list then tapered down to agriculture and farming, which contributed a mere $63,454.

To these advertisers the cost of using the air waves is formidable. To plug the drug Anacin, for example, $740,627 was spent in a single month just for time on the air, apart from talent and production costs. One competitor, Bayer Aspirin, spent $527,855 and another, Bufferin, $455,934.

IV. INDEX

None Available

V. BIBLIOGRAPHY (Representative Page)

BIBLIOGRAPHY

An asterisk (*) preceding a reference indicates that the article or a part of it has been reprinted in this book.

BOOKS AND PAMPHLETS

Abbot, Waldo and Rider, Richard. Handbook of broadcasting. McGraw. New York. '57.

Ace, Goodman. Book of little knowledge. Simon & Schuster. New York. '55.

Allen, Fred. Treadmill to oblivion. Little. Boston. '54.

Allen, Steve. Funny men. Simon & Schuster. New York. '56.

Allport, G. W. and Cantril, Hadley. Psychology of radio. Harper. New York. '35.

Bailey, K. V. Listening schools. British Broadcasting Corporation. London. '57.

Barnouw, Erik. Mass communication: television, radio, film, press. Rinehart. New York. '56.

Bellaire, Arthur. TV advertising; a handbook of modern practice. Harper. New York. '59.

Bendick, Jeanne and Bendick, Robert. Television works like this. McGraw. New York. '59.

Bluem, A. W. and others. Television in the public interest. Hastings House. New York. '61.

Blum, D. C. Pictorial history of TV. Chilton. Philadelphia. '58.

Bogart, Leo. Age of television. Ungar. New York. '58.

Brennen, Ed. Advertising media. McGraw. New York. '51.

Bryson, Lyman. Communication of ideas. Harper. New York. '48.

Bryson, Lyman. Time for reason. George W. Stewart. New York. '48.

Callahan, Jennie. Television in school, college, and community. McGraw. New York. '53.

Cassirer, H. R. Television teaching today. UNESCO. Paris. '60. (Distributed by International Documents Service. Columbia University Press. New York)

Chester, Giraud and Garrison, G. R. Television and radio; an introduction. Appleton. New York. '60.

Cogley, John. Report on blacklisting. 2v. Fund for the Republic. 133 E. 54th St. New York 22. '56.
    V 2, Radio, television.

Cooley, Hazel. Vision in television. Channel Press. New York. '52.

Crosby, John. Out of the blue. Simon and Schuster. New York. '52.

VI. BOOK REVIEWS

None Available

Taking Notes

After you have evaluated sources for relevance and reliability, you can begin to read and then take notes on the material that you have found to be relevant to your purposes. You will probably not read entire books or even entire periodical articles, but will restrict your reading to the part or parts which you will be able to use. Be sure, however, to read enough of the source to understand the context in which the author is presenting the information.

The system that you use to take notes is a matter of personal preference and convenience. The system most often recommended involves the use of 3×5 or 4×6 note cards. If used effectively, this system allows you to take notes on a wide variety of topics related to your research paper subject, to arrange your cards so that those which contain information on similar topics are placed together, and then to write your essay entirely from your note cards, following the order in which you arrange the topics.

1 Note Cards

Each note card should contain the following information:

1) the **specific** topic of the note on the card, so that you can tell at a glance what information each card contains;
2) bibliographic information to tell where you got the information;
3) the note itself, in the form of quotation, paraphrase, or summary.

The question which occurs more often than how to take notes is: What should I take notes on? Write down anything (including your thoughts which occur as you research) that you think provides relevant support for the topics of your paper or essay. This means that (1) you will take more notes than you will actually use and (2) you must have a clear idea of the topics you will address. Refer to your working outline. Don't start taking notes until you know what you are looking for.

Understanding the rationale behind the use of quotation, paraphrase, and summary can help you decide what to take notes on.

2 Quotation

Quotation is a direct, verbatim copying of a word, phrase, sentence, or passage with quotation marks placed around that which is copied. Quotation should be used sparingly (not more than 10% of your essay should be quoted). It should be used **only** for emphasis: (1) when the language and phrasing used by the author is particularly effective or striking and (2) when the author you are quoting is the (or one of the) foremost authorities and his directly quoted ideas would add credibility to your views.

3   Paraphrase

Paraphrase captures the meaning of a phrase, sentence, or passage in your own words and in approximately the same number of words as that which is being paraphrased. Since use of quotation should be limited, paraphrase is often employed in place of quotation. It should be used to capture the information in relatively short passages (three or four sentences) when that information is not especially quotable.

4   Summary

Summary captures the main ideas of longer passages (paragraphs, chapters, entire articles) in your own words and in condensed form. The length of your summary depends on the length of the original passage and/or on your intended use of the summary. You can summarize an entire book in ten words or in several hundred words, depending on how you intend to use the summary. The rationale behind the use of summary and quotation differs, since quotation is employed to emphasize a specific statement or thought, while summary is employed to capture the essence of a longer passage.

Be aware that in paraphrasing or summarizing you might use quotation. That is, you might want to emphasize a key word or phrase found in the material you are paraphrasing or summarizing. If so, place quotation marks around that word or phrase.

5   Sample Note Cards

Winn, Marie. *The Plug-In Drug.* New York: Viking Press, 1977

Original Source:

116   TELEVISION AND THE CHILD

Given the evidence that environmental experience affects brain development in definable, measurable ways, and that early experience is more influential than later experience, it seems inevitable that the television experience, which takes up so many hours of a child's waking day, must have some effects upon his brain development. And yet children's brains cannot be dissected and examined to satisfy a scientist's curiosity. Nor can animal experiments cast reliable light on questions dealing with mental functions peculiar to the human species, such as thinking or verbalizing.

Nevertheless, the fact that the brain of a young child is different in important ways from an adult brain my help us to localize the areas of neurological impact of the television experience. For it will be in those *changing* areas that any neurological change will presumably occur.

Such an area of difference between the child's and the adult's brain is precisely that of brain-hemisphere specialization, and the balance that exists between verbal and nonverbal forms of mental organization. It is here that the television experience may prove to have its greatest impact.

This is not to suggest that television viewing will prevent a normal child from learning to speak. Only in cases of gross deprivation where children are almost totally isolated from human sounds will they not proceed according to a fairly universal language-learning schedule and fail to acquire the rudiments of speech.

It is not the child's actual acquisition of language but his *commitment* to language as a means of expression and to the verbal mode as the ultimate source of fulfillment that is at stake, a commitment that may have a physiological basis in the balance of right- and left-hemisphere development.

For a young child in the process of developing those basic mental structures, concepts, and understandings required to achieve his highest potential as a rational human being, a child who has only recently made the transition from nonverbal to verbal thought, much depends upon his opportunities to exercise his growing verbal skills. The greater the child's verbal opportunities, the greater the likelihood that his language will grow in complexity and his rational, verbal thinking abilities will sharpen. The fewer his opportunities, the greater the likelihood that certain linguistic areas will remain undeveloped or underdeveloped as critical time periods come and go.

To a grown-up, nonverbal mental activities carry connotations of relaxation from the ardors of normal logical thinking and promise a much-sought-after achievement of peace and serenity. But to a young child in his formative, language-learning years, any extended regression into nonverbal mental functioning such as the television experience offers must be seen as a potential setback. As the child takes in television words and images hour after hour, day after day, with little of the mental effort that forming his own thoughts and feelings and molding them into words would require, as he *relaxes* year after year, a pattern emphasizing nonverbal cognition becomes established.

For unlike the tired businessman or professional woman or harried housewife who turns on the television set to "unwind," the young child has a built-in need for mental activity. He is a learning machine, an "absorbent mind," a glutton for experience. In a culture that depends upon a precise and effective use of spoken and written language, his optimal development requires not merely adequate, but abundant opportunities to manipulate, to learn, to synthesize experience. It is his parents, fatigued by his incessant demands for learning in the broadest sense of the word (learning that may involve whining, screaming, throwing things, pestering), who require the "relaxation" afforded by setting him before the television screen and causing him to become, once again, the passive captive of his own sensations he was when nonverbal thought was his only means of learning.

Summary Card:

Effect of T. V. on Children:
Deprivation of Verbal Skills   Winn pp. 46-47

    Marie Winn asserts that while T. V. watching
affords adults relaxation, it prevents a child
from developing the verbal skills necessary
"to achieve his highest potential as a
rational human being."

Sapir, Edward. *Language: An Introduction to the Study of Speech.* New York: Harcourt
Brace, 1921.

Original Source:

14   LANGUAGE

of view of language, thought may be defined as the highest latent or
potential content of speech, the content that is obtained by interpreting
each of the elements in the flow of language as possessed of its very fullest
conceptual value. From this it follows at once that language and thought
are not strictly coterminous. At best language can but be the outward
facet of thought on the highest, most generalized, level of symbolic
expression. To put our viewpoint somewhat differently, language is
primarily a pre-rational function. It humbly works up to the thought that
is latent in, that may eventually be read into, its classifications and its
forms; it is not, as is generally but naïvely assumed, the final label put
upon the finished thought.

Most people, asked if they can think without speech, would probably
answer, "Yes, but it is not easy for me to do so. Still I know it can be done."
Language is but a garment! But what if language is not so much a
garment as a prepared road or groove? It is, indeed, in the highest degree
likely that language is an instrument originally put to uses lower than the
conceptual plane and that thought arises as a refined interpretation of its
content. The product grows, in other words, with the instrument, and
thought may be no more conceivable, in its genesis and daily practice,
without speech than is mathematical reasoning practicable without the
lever of an appropriate mathematical symbolism. No one believes that
even the most difficult mathematical proposition is inherently dependent
on an arbitrary set of symbols, but it is impossible to suppose that the

human mind is capable of arriving at or holding such a proposition without the symbolism. The writer, for one, is strongly of the opinion that the feeling entertained by so many that they can think, or even reason, without language is an illusion. The illusion seems to be due to a number of factors. The simplest of these is the failure to distinguish between imagery and thought. As a matter of fact, no sooner do we try to put an image into conscious relation with another than we find ourselves slipping into a silent flow of words. Thought may be a natural domain apart from the artificial one of speech, but speech would seem to be the only road we know of that leads to it. A still more fruitful source of the illusive feeling that language may be dispensed with in thought is the common failure to realize that language is not identical with its auditory symbolism. The auditory symbolism may be replaced, point for point, by a motor or by a visual symbolism (many people can read, for instance, in a purely visual sense, that is, without the intermediating link of an inner flow of the auditory images that correspond to the printed or written words) or by still other, more subtle and elusive, types of transfer that are not so easy to define. Hence the contention that one thinks without language merely because he is not aware of a coexisting auditory imagery is very far indeed from being a valid one. One may go so far as to suspect that the symbolic expression of thought may in some cases run along outside the fringe of the conscious mind, so that the feeling of a free, nonlinguistic stream of thought is for minds of a certain type a relatively, but only a relatively, justified one. Psycho-physically, this would mean that the auditory or equivalent visual or motor centers in the brain, together with the appropriate paths of association, that are the cerebral equivalent of speech, are touched off so lightly during the process of thought as not to rise into consciousness at all. This would be a limiting case—thought riding lightly on the submerged crests of speech,

Quotation Card:

Correlation Between Thought and Language Sapir, pp 14-15

In an early, important study on language, Edward Sapir "is strongly of the opinion that the feeling entertained by so many that they can think ... without language is an illusion" and that "speech would seem to be the only road we know of that leads to it [thought]."

Paraphrase Card:

Correlation Between Thought and Language   Sapir, pp 14-15

   In 1921, Edward Sapir expressed his belief
that verbal skills and the ability to think
are related inasmuch as speech appears
to be "the only road we know of that leads
to it [thought]."

6   Discussion of Sample Note Cards

Note the following about the three note cards:

1) Each card has a topic in the upper left-hand corner telling specifically what information is found on the card.

2) Each card contains (in the upper right-hand corner) the last name of the author from whose text the note was taken and the page number(s) where the information can be found in the original source. If you have compiled a working bibliography, you will already have the other bibliographic information (author's full name, title, and publication information) that you will need to write endnotes and a bibliography page. If you haven't compiled a working bibliography, you should record all pertinent bibliographic information on your note card. Also, if you are using more than one work by an author, put the title of the source on the card in addition to the author's name; likewise, if two or more of the authors you will be referring to share the same last name, use first names as well as last names.

3) The summary card condenses a large amount of material (in the same card, the thoughts contained in two paragraphs are captured on the same card).

4) Summary might be used to include material that is not the most authoritative. It might, for example, relate the opinions of a writer

who is not necessarily acknowledged as an authority but whose ideas reveal that someone else believes as you do.

5) Quotation and paraphrase cards capture specific information which you want to emphasize. In the case of the sample cards, the note taker demonstrates the importance of Edward Sapir's studies on language by quoting and paraphrasing a specific idea.

6) Summary and paraphrase cards can contain quoted words and phrases. In fact, you must use quotation marks whenever you copy an author's phrasing verbatim.

7) Quotation cards require quotation marks so that you don't forget that the note is a quotation and inadvertently plagiarize.

8) Ellipsis periods (three spaced periods) are used in a direct quotation whenever words are omitted from whatever you quote (see card 2).

9) Brackets are used to add material into a quotation in order to clarify meaning (see cards 2 & 3).

10) Each note card contains a lead-in which introduces the summary, quotation, and paraphrase (e.g., Marie Winn asserts . . .). Since you will use such lead-ins in your essay, get in the habit of including them on your note cards.

Note Taking   **Exercise 2**

Using the passages provided in the exercise on source evaluation, write up one note card for each of the three sources you judged to be reliable and relevant. Remember, as was the case in the source evaluation exercise, you are looking for factual information concerning (1) the amount of money spent on and generated by commercials and (2) the resulting negative control that advertisers can hold over television programming.

Write your own note cards: one quotation card, one paraphrase card, and one summary card. Select the representative passages carefully, based on your understanding of the different rationales behind quotation, paraphrase, and summary. Keep your research needs in mind and pay attention to the nature of the information presented in each passage.

Incorporation of Notes

When you write your essay, you should not simply string together a list of quotations, paraphrases, and summaries. Your essay should principally contain your own writing, with occasional quotes, paraphrases, and summaries to help you support your ideas—the ideas you had before you began your research along with those you gained as a result of your research. Therefore, you must be able to effectively integrate the information on your cards into your own writing.

---

1 Quotation

A. **Short Quotes.** If you adhere to the rationale behind the use of quotations, most of the quotations you incorporate into your essay will be short and can be blended into your own sentences. Note, for example, the following:

```
Professor John Smith of the Boston Institute of

Astrophysics asserts that "the chance of there being

life on other planets is great."¹
```

When you integrate short quotations you must be careful not to misrepresent the author. Suppose Professor Smith really said, *"Therefore, if I were to say that the chance of there being life on other planets is great, I would be an idiot."* Your quotation would be accurate but it would be taken out of context and would misrepresent Professor Smith.

B. **Long Quotes.** At times you will have to use a longer quote of two sentences or more. In such cases, you would incorporate the quote by setting it off from your text. Note the following example:

```
    Many experts adhere to the position so em-

phatically stated by Professor John Smith of the

Boston Institute of Astrophysics:

        In all the years that we have studied

        outer space, we have not found one shred

        of evidence that life as we know it
```

exists on other planets. Therefore, if
I were to say that the chance of there
being life on other planets is great, I
would be an idiot. The atmospheric conditions in outer space simply will not
support life.[1]

In this example, the long quotation is set off from the body of the text by *triple* spaces between it and the text, and a wider indentation of *ten* spaces from the left-hand margin; the long quotation is still double-spaced, but no quotation marks are used.

When integrating either short or long quotations, remember (1) to use a lead-in introducing the quotation and establishing a context for it and (2) to document the quotation using the method prescribed by your instructor. The two methods described here (see Documentation, pp. 281–88) are those approved by the Modern Language Association (MLA) and the American Psychological Association (APA).

---

2   Paraphrase & Summary

When integrating either a paraphrase or a summary into your writing, do the following:

1) Use a lead-in to establish a context and to distinguish your voice from the voice of the author you are paraphrasing or summarizing. If, for example, you have a ten-sentence paragraph in your essay and only the last or tenth sentence is a represented summary, the reader of your essay would have no way of knowing how many sentences in the paragraph were part of the summary unless you used a lead-in to the tenth sentence.
2) Use quotation marks around key words or phrases if you take them verbatim from the author you are paraphrasing or summarizing.
3) Document paraphrases and summaries using the method prescribed by your instructor.

NAME _____ DATE _____

Using the notes you took in the Exercise on Note Taking, write a paragraph in the space provided below. State a topic sentence which synthesizes the information on your note cards, by relating the idea of the unhealthy alliance between big business and television companies. Then illustrate what you mean by *unhealthy alliance*, integrating the factual information from your note cards into your paragraph as support or evidence.

Documentation (MLA Style)

After you have written your research paper, your responsibility is to inform the reader where the information you used can be found and where further information on your subject is available. You provide such information in footnotes or endnotes and in a bibliography.

1   Footnotes/Endnotes

As the name implies, footnotes are notes found at the foot of a page of text. The notes most frequently refer the reader to the exact location of every quotation, paraphrase, or summary you use in your essay. In your text, after you incorporate material from another source, place a number, raised a half space above the line, starting with number 1 and continuing consecutively through as many numbers as needed. These numbers refer the reader to your notes, where you repeat the number and tell where you found the information to which the number refers.

It is common practice now to put the notes on a separate page at the end of the research paper rather than at the bottom of pages in the text. The notes are then referred to as endnotes and the page on which they occur should be entitled **Notes.**

2   Bibliography

A bibliography is a list of sources wherein the reader of the paper can find information on the subject you have written on. This list is to be alphabetized by the last names of the authors and will be the concluding section of your paper. As you may notice in your research, bibliographies are often extensive, including many more works than are cited in a book or article. Generally, however, you are asked to list only those works you actually use (i.e., quote, paraphrase, or summarize from) in your paper. In such a case, the bibliographic page is more appropriately entitled **Works Cited.**

3   Footnote/Endnote and Bibliography Form

Below you will find an example of the footnote and bibliography form approved by MLA. The chart which illustrates the difference between endnote and bibliography form and the models for them are drawn from Edward P. J. Corbett's *Little English Handbook,* 4th Edition.

Bibliography Form

Ryan, Edwin. *A College Handbook to Newman.* Washington, DC: Catholic Education Press, 1930.

Endnote Form

[8]Edwin Ryan, *A College Handbook to Newman* (Washington, DC: Catholic Education Press, 1930), p. 109.

Note that the two forms differ in the following ways:

BIBLIOGRAPHY	ENDNOTE
(a) The first line begins at the left-hand margin, with all subsequent lines indented.	**(a)** The first line is indented, with all subsequent lines brought out to the left-hand margin.
(b) The name of the author is inverted (last name first) for purposes of alphabetizing the list of entries.	**(b)** The name of the author is set down in the normal order.
(c) The three main divisions (author, title and publishing data) are separated by periods.	**(c)** The three main divisions (author, title, and publishing data) are separated by commas.
(d) Place of publication, name of the publisher, and publication date follow the title, without parentheses.	**(d)** Place of publication, name of the publisher, and publication date are enclosed in parentheses.
(e) The subtitle, if any, should be included in the citation. See (2) below.	**(e)** The subtitle, if any, may be omitted in the citation.
(f) There is no page reference unless the entry is for an article or part of a collection, in which case the full span of pages (first page and last page) is cited.	**(f)** Only a specific page reference is cited.

On certain occasions, the information contained in the examples above might have to be supplemented with additional pertinent information. Examine the models listed below for variant forms of book entries and for periodical and newspaper entries.

(1) A single book by a single author:

Seki, Hozen. *The Great Natural Way.* New York: American Buddhist Academy, 1976.

[14]Hozen Seki, *The Great Natural Way* (New York: American Buddhist Academy, 1976), p. 88.

(2) A single book by more than one author:

Baran, Paul A., and Paul M. Sweezy. *Monopoly Capital: An Essay on American Economic and Social Order.* New York: Monthly Review Press, 1966.

[12]Paul A. Baran and Paul M. Sweezy, *Monopoly Capital* (New York: Monthly Review Press, 1966), p. 392.

(3) A book of more than one volume:

Hays, William Lee, and Robert L. Winkler. *Statistics: Probability, Inference, and Decision.* 2 vols. New York: Holt, Rinehart & Winston, 1970.

[13]William Lee Hays and Robert L. Winkler, *Statistics: Probability, Inference, and Decision* (New York: Holt, Rinehart & Winston, 1970), II, 137.

(4) A book edited by one or more editors:

Essays in American Economic History. Ed. Alfred W. Coats and Ross M. Robertson. London: Edward Arnold, 1969.

[3]*Essays in American Economic History,* ed. Alfred W. Coats and Ross M. Robertson (London: Edward Arnold, 1969), pp. 268-9.

(5) An essay or a chapter by an author in an edited collection:

Svaglic, Martin J. "Classical Rhetoric and Victorian Prose." *The Art of Victorian Prose.* Ed. George Levine and William Madden. New York: Oxford Univ. Press, 1968, pp. 268–88.

[2]Martin J. Svaglic, "Classical Rhetoric and Victorian Prose," *The Art of Victorian Prose,* ed. George Levine and William Madden (New York: Oxford Univ. Press, 1968), pp. 268–70.

(6) A new edition of a book:

Doughty, Oswald. *A Victorian Romantic, Dante Gabriel Rossetti.* 2nd ed. London: Oxford Univ. Press, 1960.

[5]Oswald Doughty, *A Victorian Romantic, Dante Gabriel Rossetti,* 2nd ed. (London: Oxford Univ. Press, 1960), p. 35.

(7) A book that is part of a series:

Heytesbury, William. *Medieval Logic and the Rise of Mathematical Physics.* University of Wisconsin Publications in Medieval Science, No. 3. Madison: Univ. of Wisconsin Press, 1956.

[26]William Heytesbury, *Medieval Logic and the Rise of Mathematical Physics*. University of Wisconsin Publications in Medieval Science, No. 3 (Madison: Univ. of Wisconsin Press, 1956), p. 97.

(8) A Government Bulletin or Pamphlet:

U.S. Department of Health, Education, and Welfare, *Industrial Pollutants*. Washington, D.C.: Government Printing Office, 1978.

[18]U.S. Dept. of Health, Education, and Welfare, *Industrial Pollutants* (Washington, D.C.: Government Printing Office, 1978), p. 24.

(9) A Film, a Radio Program, or a Television Program:

The Member of the Wedding. With Pearl Bailey, Dana Hill, and Howard Rollins. Writ. Carson McCullers. Dir. Delbert Mann. NBC Live Theater. NBC, 20 December 1982.

[11]*The Member of the Wedding*, with Pearl Bailey, Dana Hill, and Howard Rollins, writ. Carson McCullers, dir. Delbert Mann, NBC Live Theater, NBC, 20 Dec. 1982.

(10) A signed article from an encyclopedia:

Ewing, J. A. "Steam-Engine and Other Heat-Engines." *Encyclopaedia Britannica*. 9th ed., XXII, 473–526.

[4]J. A. Ewing, "Steam-Engine and Other Heat-Engines," *Encyclopaedia Britannica*, 9th ed., XXII, 475–7.

(11) An article from a journal:

Adkins, Nelson. "Emerson and the Bardic Tradition." *Publications of the Modern Language Association*, 72 (1948), 662–7.

[12]Nelson Adkins, "Emerson and the Bardic Tradition," *PMLA*, 72 (1948), 665.

(12) An article in a popular magazine:

Levin, Robert J. "Sex, Morality, and Society." *Saturday Review*, 9 July 1966, pp. 29–30.

[4]Robert J. Levin, "Sex, Morality, and Society," *Saturday Review*, 9 July 1966, p. 29.

(13) A signed article in a newspaper:

Gilman, Art. "Altering U. S. Flag for Political Causes Stirs a Legal Debate." *Wall Street Journal*, 12 June 1970, p. 1.

[15]Art Gilman, "Altering U.S. Flag for Political Causes Stirs a Legal Debate," *Wall Street Journal*, 12 June 1970, p. 1.

(14) A signed book review:

Dalbor, John B. Review of *Meaning and Mind: A Study in the Psychology of Language*, by Robert F. Terwilliger. *Philosophy & Rhetoric*, 5 (1972), 60–61.

[19]John F. Dalbor, rev. of *Meaning and Mind: A Study in the Psychology of Language*, by Robert F. Terwilliger, *Philosophy & Rhetoric*, 5 (1972), 60–61.

(15) A Personal Letter or Interview:

Glenn, Senator John. Letter to author. 20 June 1983.

[12]Letter received from Senator John Glenn, 20 June 1983.

Documentation (APA Style)

If you are writing a research paper for a course in the social sciences (education, psychology, sociology, etc.), you may be asked to use the American Psychological Association (APA) system of documenting. If so, your goal is still, as it is with the MLA system, to inform the reader of your paper where the information you use from other written sources can be found and where further information on your subject can be found.

1 Notes

With the APA style, instead of using the MLA numbering system for your notes, you will use an internal form of documentation. That is, after a quotation, paraphrase, or summary from a source, put in parentheses the author's last name, the publication date of the work, and sometimes the page number(s) on which the information is found.

2 APA Form

Below you will find examples of the APA system of documenting.

(a) If a whole work is being referred to, only the author's last name and the date of the work are given in parentheses.

```
A recent study has confirmed that twelve-year-

olds grow at an amazingly rapid rate (Swanson, 1969).
```

(b) A page number or a chapter number is supplied only if part of a work is being referred to. Quotations always demand the addition of a page number.

```
The committee boldly declared that "morality

could not be enforced, but it could be bought"

(Dawson, 1975, p. 105).
```

(c) Any information supplied in the text itself need not be repeated in the parentheses.

```
Anderson (1948) found that only middle-class

Europeans disdained our cultural values.
```

In 1965, Miller professed his fervent admira-

tion of our admissions policy.

(d) If a work has two authors, both authors should be cited each time
a reference is made to that text. If a work has three or more
authors, all the authors should be cited the first time, but
subsequently only the name of the first author followed by **et al.**
needs to be given.

The circulation of false rumors poisoned the

environment of that conference (Getty & Howard, 1979).

The overall effect of the smear tactics was a

marked decline in voter registrations (Abraham,

Davis & Keppler, 1952).

In three successive national elections, voters

from Slavic neighborhoods showed a 72% turnout

(Abraham et al., 1952, pp. 324-327).

(e) If several works are cited at the same point in the text, the works
should be arranged alphabetically according to the last name of the
author and should be separated with semicolons.

All the studies of the problem agree that the

proposed remedy is worse than the malady (Brown

& Turkell, 1964; Firkins, 1960; Howells, 1949;

Jackson, Miller, & Naylor, undated; Kameron, in

press).

(f) If several works by the same author are cited in the same
reference, the works are distinguished by the publication dates,
arranged in chronological order and separated with commas. Two
or more works published by the same author in the same year are
distinguished by the letters **a, b, c,** etc., added to the repeated date.
In such chronological listings, works "in press" are always listed last.

3   Bibliography or References

The APA system is also slightly different from the MLA system in the format of the bibliographic entries. Your bibliographic page should be entitled **References** or **Works Cited** and will include *only* those works quoted from, paraphrased from, or summarized in your paper. You still alphabetize your list of works by the last name of the author cited, but then the MLA rules involving the first names of authors, multiple authors, capitalization, punctuation, and sequence of information are altered.

4   APA Reference Form

Below you will find examples of the APA bibliographic format.

(1) A book by a single author:

> Luria, A. R. The working brain: An introduc-
>
> tion to neuro-psychology. London: Penguin,
>
> 1973.

Note that the title of the book is underlined but that only the first word of the title and the first word following the colon in the title are capitalized. (Any proper nouns in a title would also be capitalized; see the following example.) The three main parts of an entry—author, title, and publication data—are separated with periods.

(2) A book by several authors:

> Koslin, S., Koslin, B. L., Pargament, R., &
>
> Pendelton, S. An evaluation of fifth grade
>
> reading programs in ten New York City com-
>
> munity School Districts, 1973-1974. New
>
> York: Riverside Research Institute, 1975.

Note that the names of all the authors are inverted, that the names are separated with commas, and that an ampersand (&) is put before the last name in the series (even when there are only two names; see the following example.)

(3) An article in an edited collection:

Bobrow, D. G., & Norman, D. A.   Some principles

of memory schemata.   In D. G. Bobrow & A. M.

Collins (Eds.), <u>Representation</u> <u>and</u> <u>under-</u>

<u>standing</u>: <u>Studies</u> <u>in</u> <u>cognitive</u> <u>science</u>.   New

York: Academic Press, 1975.

Note that the title of the article (**Some principles** etc.) is not enclosed in quotation marks and that only the first word of this title is capitalized. (Any proper nouns in the title of the article would, of course, be capitalized.) Note also that the subsequent names of the two editors (**Eds.**) **of the collection are not inverted and that there is no comma between the names.**

(4) An article in a journal:

Stahl, A.   The structure of children's composi-

tions: Developmental and ethnic differences.

<u>Research</u> <u>in</u> <u>the</u> <u>Teaching</u> <u>of</u> <u>English</u>, 1977,

<u>11</u>, 156–163.

Note that all substantive words in the title of the journal are capitalized and that the title of the journal is underlined. Note also that the year comes before the volume number and that the volume number (*11*) is underlined. For a journal that begins the numbering of its pages with page 1 in each issue, the number of the issue should be indicated with an Arabic number following the volume number—*11*(**3**).

(5) A book by a corporate author:

American Psychological Association.   <u>Standards</u>

<u>for</u> <u>educational</u> <u>and</u> <u>psychological</u> <u>tests</u> <u>and</u>

<u>manuals</u>.   Washington, DC: Author, 1966.

Books and articles with corporate authors are listed alphabetically according to the first significant word of the entry (here **American**). The word **Author** listed with the publication data indicates that the publisher of the work is the same as the group named in the author slot. If, however, the publisher is different from the corporate author, the name of that publisher would be given right after the place of publication.

NAME _____ DATE _____

Below, you are given bibliographic information about ten different sources. Arrange the information into proper MLA endnote form and bibliographic form on your own paper. You must put the information in the correct order and supply proper punctuation. Also, each set of information _might_ contain material which should not be included in your endnote or bibliographic entry.

1. Title of Book: Socialization Through the Ages
   Author: Helen Adams
   Edition: 1st ed.
   Page: 127
   Date of Publication: 1980
   Publisher: Rising Moon Press
   Place of Publication: Caldwell, Idaho

2. Title of Periodical: Sociological Issues
   Volume Number: 24
   Title of Article: Personality Development in
                               Early School Years
   General Editor of Periodical: Jonas Schiller
   Author of Article: Donald Smithson
   Pages on which Article Appears: 123–30
   Date: Fall, 1960

3. Title of Newspaper: Lincoln City Register [Oregon]
   Date: July 15, 1981
   Author: None given
   Title of Article: Schools Set Discipline Code for
                               Students
   Page: 1

4. Title of Periodical: Times Weekly
   Volume Number: 158
   Date: November 5, 1982
   Title of Article: Peer Pressure in the Schools
   Author: Not given
   Pages on which Article Appears: 80–85

NAME _____ DATE _____

5. Title of Book: Socialization
   Editor: James Hamilton
   Title of Essay: The Movement of the Child
                               from Family into Society
   Author: Donna Chapman
   Date of Publication: 1978
   Publisher: Johnson and Company
   Place of Publication: Los Angeles, California
   Page: 347–367

6. Title of Government Bulletin: Child Abuse and Criminal
                               Behavior
   Government Agency: U.S. Department of Justice
   Number of Pages: 192
   Date of Publication: 1982
   Publisher: Government Printing Office
   Place of Publication: Washington, D. C.

7. Date of Interview: August 3, 1983
   Kind of Interview: Personal
   Interviewer: Timothy Cranston
   Interviewee: California State Representative
                               Miles Lipscomb
   Subject of Interview: Child Welfare Laws

8. Title of Television Program: Whose Kids Are These?:
                               Children of Working Parents
   Date of Telecast: February 19, 1982
   Television Network: CBS
   Moderator: James Stanley

9. Date of Letter: April 12, 1981
   Recipient of Letter: Timothy Cranston
   Sender of Letter: Wilson B. Knowles
   Title of Sender: Assistant Professor of Sociology
                               at Wayne State University

10. Title of Article: Child Development
    Pages on Which Article Appears: 512–525
    Title of Encyclopedia: Encyclopedia of Sociology
    Author of Article: Peter Franklin
    Place of Publication: New York
    Volume: I
    Edition: 1981, 3rd

**Below you are given bibliographic information about five
different sources. Arrange the information into the proper
APA form as you would present it on your References page.
You must put the information in the correct order and supply
the proper punctuation. Also, each set of information *might*
contain material which should not be included in the entry.**

1. Title of Book: Socialization Through the Ages
   Author: Helen Adams
   Edition: 1st
   Date of Publication: 1980
   Publisher: Rising Moon Press
   Place of Publication: Caldwell, Idaho

2. Title of Journal: Sociological Issues
   Volume Number: 24
   Title of Article: Personality Development in
                                         Early School Years
   General Editor of Journal: Jonas Schiller
   Author of Article: Donald Smithson
   Pages on which Article Appears: 123–130
   Date: 1960

3. Title of Book: The Nuclear Family
   Date of Publication: 1977
   Author: The Association of International
                                         Psychologists
   Publisher: The Association of International
                                         Psychologists
   Place of Publication: San Francisco, California

4. Title of Journal: Child Development
   Volume Number: 35
   Date: 1982
   Title of Article: Peer Pressure in the Schools
   Authors: Nancy Byron and James Wilson
   Pages on which Article Appears: 80–85

5. Title of Book: Socialization
   Editor: James Hamilton
   Title of Essay: The Movement of the Child
                               from Family into Society
   Author: Donna Chapman
   Date of Publication: 1978
   Publisher: Johnson and Company
   Place of Publication: Los Angeles, California
   Pages on which Essay Appears: 219–251

Index